On Wo......

Born in Punjab's Hadali village (now in Pakistan) in 1915, Khushwant Singh has acquired an iconic stature: he is, arguably, India's best-known and most widely read author, columnist and journalist. He was founder-editor of *Yojana*, and editor of *The Illustrated Weekly of India*, *National Herald* and the *Hindustan Times*. His first book, *The Mark of Vishnu and Other Stories*, was published in 1950. The best known among these are the novels *Train to Pakistan*, *I Shall Not Hear the Nightingale* and *Delhi*; his autobiography, *Truth, Love and a Little Malice*; and the two-volume *A History of the Sikhs*.

Khushwant Singh was member of the Rajya Sabha from 1980 to 1986. He was awarded the Padma Bhushan in 1974; he returned the award in 1984 to protest the siege of the Golden Temple by the Indian Army. In 2007, he was awarded India's second highest civilian honour, the Padma Vibhushan.

Khushwant Singh died in 2014.

On
Women

~ SELECTED WRITINGS ~

KHUSHWANT SINGH

RUPA

Published by
Rupa Publications India Pvt. Ltd 2014
7/16, Ansari Road, Daryaganj
New Delhi 110002

Sales centres:
Allahabad Bengaluru Chennai
Hyderabad Jaipur Kathmandu
Kolkata Mumbai

ISBN: 978-81-291-2492-0

10 9 8 7 6 5 4 3 2 1

First impression 2014

Typeset in IowanOldST BT by SÜRYA, New Delhi
Printed at Replika Press Pvt. Ltd., India

CONTENTS

❧

CONTENTS

GEORGINE

〜

It had been a bad year for me. I didn't have many writing assignments and the articles I sold to Indian papers did not get me enough to maintain the lifestyle I was accustomed to. So I registered myself as a guide with the Tourist Department of the Government of India and left my card at foreign embassies and international organizations. During the tourist season between October and March I made quite a bit in tips in foreign currency which I exchanged for rupees at rates higher than the official. I earned commissions from hotels, curio dealers and astrologers for the custom I brought them. Men left me the remains of their bottle of Scotch. Sometimes middle-aged women invited me to their rooms and gave me presents for the services I rendered them.

It was not very hard work. After I had memorized the names of a few dynasties and emperors and the years when they ruled, all I had to do was to pick up a few anecdotes to spice my stories. At the Qutub Minar I told them of the number of suicides that had taken place and how no one could jump clear of the tower and come down in one piece. I told them of Humayun's father, Babar, going around his son's sickbed four times, praying to Allah to transfer his son's illness to him, and how Humayun had been restored to health and Babar died a few days later. About the Red Fort and its palaces, I had picked up a lot of interesting details: from the time Shah Jahan had built it, the kings who had sat on the Peacock Throne and were later blinded or murdered; the British who had taken it after the Mutiny of 1857; the trials of INA officers, down to 15 August 1947 when Lord Mountbatten had lowered the Union Jack and Nehru hoisted the Indian tricolour on the ramparts. Once having done my homework, there was little more to do than impress the tourists with my learning.

After a while I began to enjoy my work.

Although I did not find anyone who would give me a free round-the-world ticket, I could boast that the world came to me. Once a cousin who had found a job as a worker in England told me of the number of white girls he had 'killed'. They were English girls working in the same factory. I told him that I had 'killed' many more Europeans, Americans, Japanese, Arabs and Africans, sitting where I was in Delhi, without having to pay a counterfeit four-anna coin to anyone. The fellow began to drool at the mouth and scratch his testicles with envy.

The only thing that troubled me was that I never got a chance to make friends with anyone. All the Marys, Janes, Francoises and Mikis darlinged and honeyed me for a day or two and then vanished forever. After a few weeks I could not recall their names or faces. All I could recollect was the way they had behaved when I bestrode them. Some had been as lifeless as the bed on which we lay; some had squirmed and screamed as they climaxed. A few had mouthed obscenities, slapped me on the face and told me to fuck off.

It was different with the American Missy Baba, Georgine. My contact with the US Embassy was a man named Carlyle. I do not know what he did in the embassy except that he looked after what he called 'visiting firemen'. He had tried out other guides. Once he was assured that I 'did no hanky panky' with visitors, he put a lot of custom my way.

Americans were my best customers. Despite their brash manners, they were more friendly and generous than other foreigners. I was particularly careful with Carlyle's 'visiting firemen'. I was respectful, polite and kept my distance. I opened car doors for them, did not angle for tips or look eagerly at their tape recorders, cameras and ballpoint pens. (I knew they would leave some memento for me.) I did not take them to emporia to earn commissions but helped them with their shopping at the best and cheapest stores. I never made passes at Carlyle's introductions and only obliged those who insisted on my obliging them.

My Oxbridge accent impressed Americans more than it did the other nationalities; to them I was a gentleman guide, a well-to-do fellow fallen on evil days, which was true.

Carlyle introduced me to Georgine.

Georgine was Mrs Carlyle's niece and had come to Delhi to spend her Christmas vacations, 'This is Georgine,' Carlyle said, without mentioning her second name. 'And this is your guide,' without mentioning mine. I bowed. She said 'Hi.'

As I said before, she was very young, gawky, freckled, pimpled, snub-nosed but also large-bosomed and even larger-assed. She wore a tight-fitting sweater with

'Arizona' printed across her boobs and bum-tight jeans frayed at the ends. I asked her what interested her more, people or monuments. She shrugged her shoulders, stuck out her tongue, and replied in a voice full of complaint: 'How should I know? A bit of both, I guess.' She proceeded to take snapshots of the Carlyles, the house, the car—then handed me her mini-camera so she could be in the pictures as well. She spoke very fast and dropped the g's at the end of most words: goin', comin', gettin', seein'. She was very animated and spoke with her grey eyes and hands; she interspersed her speech with noises like 'unh', and words like 'shucks' and 'crikey', and was constantly sticking out her red tongue.

'What are we waitin' for?' she demanded, turning to me the first day after she had finished the photo session.

I opened the rear door of the car for her.

She ignored me and bounced into the front seat beside the chauffeur. I took my place in the rear seat. 'Miss…'

'The name is Georgine.'

'Miss Georgine, have you…'

'Not Miss Georgine; just plain and simple Georgine, if you don't mind.'

'I was going to ask you if you had read any Indian history. We are going to see…'

'That's a stoopid question to ask an American high-school girl. Why in the name of Christ should I have read Indian history?' I decided to keep cool. We passed through Delhi Gate into Faiz Bazaar. 'What are all these jillions doin'?' she demanded.

'They are not jillions, they are vegetable-sellers. They…'

She turned round as if to make sure I was human. 'You don't know a jillion? It is the highest number—more than millions of millions. Even the dumbest American kid knows that.'

'Oh, I see,' I replied tamely. 'The population of Delhi has more than trebled in these last twenty years. It is over four million now.'

'I don't want to know that!' she snapped. We went out of Faiz Bazaar. On our left, the Royal Mosque, Jama Masjid; on our right, the massive red walls of the Fort. She ordered the chauffeur to stop and took more snapshots.

We drove up to the entrance of the Red Fort. While I queued up to buy a ticket for her, she took photographs: Chandni Chowk, the tongas, hawkers, beggars, everything. She stopped outside the entrance to take pictures of the guards, looked up at the towering walls and exclaimed, 'Gee!'

No sooner had we entered the arcade with its rows of shops aglitter with brass, gold and silver thread embroidery, miniature Taj Mahals and other bric-a-brac, than she stretched her arms wide and exclaimed, 'I want everythin' in this crummy bazaar. How much?' She went from shop to shop picking up things and putting them down with a grunt. But she was canny. She parried every attempt to sell her anything.

A marble-seller would say, 'Yes memsahib, some marbil-varbil?' and she would shake her head and reply firmly, 'No thanks.'

We came to the Naqqar Khana gate. I cleared my throat. She pulled out her *Murray's Guide* and said: 'Don't tell me. This is where drums were beaten, right? And that red buildin' in front is the Dear one somethin'-or-the-other where the kingee received common folk, right?'

'Right on the mark. It is the Diwan-i-Am, the Hall of General Audience. You don't need a guide, you know everything.'

'No. I don't,' she snapped. Armed with *Murray's Guide* she instructed me on Emperor Shah Jahan, when he had lived, when he had built the palaces, pointed out the figure of Orpheus behind the throne, the Rang Mahal, the 'Dreamin' Chamber', the octagonal Jasmine tower and the 'Dearonee...'

'Diwan-i-Khas.'

'Where kingee sat on the Peacock Throne to receive noblemen. Right?'

'Right.'

'Goodee! That pearly mosque built by the kingee's son who locked up Dad and became King Orangeade.'

'Aurangzeb.'

'Aren't I clever?'

'Very! You could make a handsome living as a professional guide.'

'I could at that! I am thirsty. Can I get a carton of milk or a Coke some place?'

'Coke, yes. Milk, no.'

We returned to the arcade. She drank two bottles of Coke, pressed her belly and belched. 'Sorree! I feel good.'

It usually took me over an hour and a half to take visitors round the Red Fort. Georgine did it in twenty minutes. I picked up a marble Taj Mahal encased in glass and nodded to the shopkeeper. He wagged his head to indicate I could have it for free. 'Miss... I mean Georgine, this is for you. With my compliments.'

'Me? What for?' she demanded, blushing.

She grabbed it from my hands and clasped it to her big bosom. 'It's lovely! Thank you.' She gave me a peck on my nose. 'And that's for you bein' so nice to a horrid girl.'

In the car this time, she took the rear seat beside me. When I asked the chauffeur to take us to the Royal Mosque, she protested: 'Nope. One mornin', one buildin'. Okay?'

'That would take us a whole month to do Delhi.'

'Goodie! You can spend every mornin' with me. Won't you like that?'

We drove through Chandni Chowk, Khari Bawli and Sadar Bazaar. Georgine kept taking snapshots and making unintelligible sounds. Then she suddenly turned round, stared at me and giggled, 'Gawd! You are a funny lookin' man!' she exclaimed. 'If somebody had told me last week that I'd be ridin' around with a darkie with a bandage round his head and a beard round his chin, I would have died.' I made no comment. She sensed my resentment. 'Don't mind me,' she added, 'I am always sayin' such dumb, stoopid things. What have you got under that bandage anyway?' I made no reply. She grunted an 'unh' and said no more till we were back in Carlyle's home. As she got out of the car she asked, 'Can I pull your beard?' Before I could raise my hand to protect myself she grabbed it in her hand and gave it a violent tug. She threw three ten-rupee notes on the seat, jumped out with the miniature Taj in her arms and, with a jerk of her big bottom, ran to the door. 'Bye! See you tomorrow.'

The bloody bitch! I muttered to myself. What she needs is to be put across the knee, her jeans ripped off and a few hard smacks on her large, melon-sized bottom. Followed by buggery.

At the Coffee House I found myself telling my cronies about Georgine. I didn't like my Sikh journalist friend referring to her as 'another quail I had trapped'. Nor the politician warning me against carnal knowledge of a girl of sixteen. When I came out of the Coffee House, it was late in the afternoon. The jamun trees were alive with the screeching of parakeets. I wanted to fill my chest and yell her name so loudly that it would be heard all over Connaught Circus, *'Georgeeen,'* and the traffic would come to a halt. *'Georgeeen'* and the parakeets would stop screaming. And the only sound to be heard would be *'Georgine, Georgine, Georgine,'* echoing round and round the Circus.

That evening I told Bhagmati about Georgine. As usual she did not like my being so enthusiastic about anyone other than her. I tried to laugh it off by reminding her that Georgine was forty years younger than me. That did not reassure her. And when I took her with greater gusto than usual, she asked, 'What is the matter with you today?' Meaning *you are not taking me but that fat-bottomed sixteen-year-old white girl.* She was right.

I was less exuberant in the morning. However, I spent twenty minutes in my cold, damp bathroom dyeing my beard. By the time I turned up at Carlyle's house, I was apprehensive of the kind of reception I would get.

Georgine was outside soaking in the sun. She looked more grown up. 'How do you like my new hairdo?' she asked, turning her head sideways. The hair was bunched on top of her head and tied in a chignon. It made her neck look longer and bared her small pink ears.

'Very nice! Makes you look like a lady.'

'I am that. Shucks!'

In the car she asked me if I slept with my turban on.

I replied: 'If you were a little older, I would have said, "Come and find out for yourself."'

Her face flushed. 'You are an ole lech! You makin' a pass at me or somethin'?'

It was my turn to be embarrassed. 'I said if you were older, and I meant a lot older. I must be older than your father.'

'I don't buy that kind of crap!'

I laid on some flattery. White people are not used to

flattery and succumb very easily. She gave me an opening by taking my hand and apologizing: 'Don't be mad with me. I don't mean to be nasty.'

'You are not nasty,' I replied, taking a grip on her hand, 'you are the nicest Missy Baba I've met.'

'Messy what?' she asked, raising her voice.

'Not messy, Missy. No flattery; it is not often I have someone as pretty to take around.'

'Unh,' she growled. 'I am not pretty or good lookin' or anythin' like that.'

But it was clear that my compliment had hit the mark. Her face had gone pink with happiness and after a pause she said, 'You're a nice ole man. Can I call you pop? I don't know your name anyhow.'

Girls are easier to seduce when they are sixteen than when they are a year or two older. At sixteen they are unsure of themselves and grateful for any reassurance you can give them about their looks or brains—either will do. Georgine, despite her brashness, proved very vulnerable. I took her to the Coffee House, as I said, 'to show her off to my friends'. She blushed again and repeated, 'You *are* an ole lech you know! But I like you.'

At the Coffee House, we sat in the section marked 'Families Only'. I ordered a Coke for her and went to greet my friends. They were not very complimentary about Georgine. Said my Sikh journalist friend: 'From the way you described her, I thought you had picked up a Marilyn Monroe. Nice fat boobs and bum though!'

'She's no Noor Jahan,' opined the political expert. 'Like any American schoolgirl. Must have a nice pussy. But you must be madder than I thought; you try any tricks with that one, you will be in for seven years' rigorous imprisonment.'

Ugly, vulgar words. I rejoined Georgine. 'What did they have to say about your girlfriend?' she asked.

'Girlfriend? Oh, you mean you?' I replied, pretending to have been taken by surprise. 'They said you were very beautiful.'

'Liar! I bet you a hundred dollars they said, "What are you doin' with a lil' girl like that? Foolin' around with anyone under seventeen can land you in jail." How 'bout that for a guess?'

'Wrong, wrong, wrong,' I protested vehemently. I could see she was happy.

This time she put my fee in an envelope and gave it to me with, 'Thanks a whole lot.'

That evening I was by turns exhilarated and conscience-stricken. In my confusion I rang her up without having anything to say to her. Her uncle picked up the phone. 'You must not let Georgine make a nuisance of herself,' he said, 'and let me have your bill for the time she's been with you.' He put down the receiver without asking me why I had called. But I was excited to know that Georgine had paid me without telling her uncle. I decided to use the information at an appropriate moment.

Meanwhile, I became bolder in my compliments. Since she changed her hairstyle every day, I got many opportunities to say things that would please her. One day she dressed herself in a bright red sari. It did not suit her, nor did she know how a woman in a sari should walk—like most Caucasians, she had a masculine stride. I said 'How charming,' and she replied, 'Oh thank you, I thought you'd sort of like to see me in your native costume.' I explained that the sari was not native to the Punjab and that a salwar-kameez would look even nicer on her. 'O great!' she exclaimed. 'I must have these thingees at once.' I took her to a tailor and while she was choosing the material, I told him in Punjabi to send the finished products, with the bill, to me. Georgine could not make up her mind. What she liked best, she said, was too expensive for her. So she settled for second best. I spoke to the tailor (again in Punjabi) to use the material of her first choice.

'You think it will look nice on me?' she asked me when we were in the car.

'I am sure it will. We have a word in our language, jamazebi, which means, the ability to fit into any clothes. I think you will look nice in anything you wear.' (Far from being jamazeb, because of her large bosom and broad hips, Georgine had difficulty in fitting into readymade clothes.) 'You are nuts,' she said, dismissing the compliment. 'I know none of the nice things you say are true, but I like you sayin' them. So don't stop, O—Kay?'

Getting her into my apartment was easy.

Two days after she had been measured, I offered to drive her around in my own car. When I went to pick her up, I said as casually as I could, 'Your things have been delivered to my apartment. Would you like to pick them up before we go sightseeing?'

'O—Kay.'

She looked around admiringly at my books and pictures. 'Nice, comfy pad,' she remarked.

'Thank you. Do sit down.'

She took off her shoes, bounced onto the settee and crossed her legs. 'Nunc! What you starin' at?'

I quoted Ghalib, first in Urdu and then translated it for her: 'She has come to my house. Sometimes I look at her, sometimes I look at my house.'

'That means you're pleased to have me here. Where are my thingees?'

I brought the bundle and untied it. 'I didn't order that one; it was too expensive, you remember? That old tailor is tryin' to rob me. All you Indians try to fleece us Americans. You think we're a bunch of suckers, don't you?'

'He's not charging you any more for this material. He knew you liked it better, so he's made it just for you.'

She was nonplussed. 'I am sorry. That's very nice of him. And this?' she asked, opening out a sequined dupatta, 'It is very pretty, but I didn't ask for this.'

'That goes with the other things. Nothing extra.'

She draped it over her head and looked around for a mirror. 'Where can I try them on?' she asked, taking the bundle under her arm. 1 showed her to my bedroom. I was left alone for some time. I poured myself a whisky and gulped it down neat. I moved from the chair to the sofa.

Georgine came out in Punjabi clothes.

The dupatta was like a small white cloud studded with stars haloing her red hair, face and shoulders. The clothes fitted her. It seemed as if she were formed to wear Punjabi clothes. 'How's that?' she asked, pirouetting on her toes.

'Very becoming! Much nicer than anything you've worn.'

'Thank you, I sort of like it too.'

She came and sat beside me on the sofa.

She opened her handbag, 'How much does he want for this?'

My voice stuck in my throat, I forced it out. 'Nothing. Allow me the privilege of making this a present. Please!'

'Thank you and all that. But I know you can't afford it.'

'Yes I can; and it'll make me very happy.'

'Okay, if it'll make you happy.' She turned around and gave me a quick kiss on my beard, 'Thank you, pop.'

The kiss paralysed my tongue. After a while I was able to say: 'And I owe you money. You paid me for the outings out of your own money, didn't you?'

'How do you know?'

'I rang up your uncle.'

She turned scarlet. 'That was a dumb thing to do! What did he say?'

I took her hand in mine. 'Don't worry. I did not tell him you had paid me. Now I can earn a double fee.'

'You cunning ole Oriental!' she laughed. 'I'm relieved to know my ole uncle doesn't know.'

'Why didn't you tell him?'

'I dunno.'

The initiative was now mine. 'Maybe you wanted to be with me without his knowing.'

'Maybe,' she replied, tossing back her hair.

Any experienced lecher knows that one should not waste words with a teenager because when it comes to real business she gets tongue-tied or can only say, 'No.' It is best to talk to her body with your hands. That excites her to a state of speechless acceptance. I ran my fingers up and down her lower arm. She watched them till goose pimples came up. Thereafter, all I had to do was to put my arm around her waist, draw her towards me and smother her lips, eyes, nose, ears and neck with kisses. She moaned helplessly. I slipped my hand under her kameez and played with her taut nipples. Then I undid her pyjama cord and slipped my fingers between her damp thighs. A little gentle ministration with my hand made her convulse and she climaxed, groaning 'O God! O God!' She lay still like a human-sized rubber doll. I put my hand on her bosom. She slapped it and pushed it away. She picked up her clothes and went to the bedroom. She came back in her jeans, tossed the bundle of salwar-kameez and sequined dupatta on the settee and strode out of the apartment.

That was the last I saw of Georgine.

And she was the last customer Carlyle put my way. I

do not know whether what I had done had amounted to having carnal knowledge of a girl below the age of consent. But for many long days and nights, I pondered over the words in the *Mahabharata*: 'As two pieces of wood floating on the ocean come together at one time and are again separated, even such is the union of living creatures in this world.'

YASMEEN

I met Yasmeen while attending classes in comparative religion in the department of religion and philosophy.

I had begun to enjoy the lectures on religion by Dr Ashby, our professor. There was a motley group of students in his class from different disciplines— medicine, literature, engineering and others. Among the thirty-odd who were regulars, there were two nuns, and a woman in salwar-kameez in her late thirties. She wore a lot of gold jewellery and was heavily made up. Since she did not wear a bindi, I presumed she was a Muslim. She sat in the front row. I was always a backbencher. After each lecture, there were discussions, and some students, the Muslim woman in the front row in particular, had much to say. I took no part in them since I knew very little about any religion.

Dr Ashby took us through the world's major religions: Zoroastrianism, Jainism, Buddhism, Judaism, Hinduism, Christianity and Islam. I was most interested in hearing what he had to say about Hinduism. Despite being a Hindu, I knew almost nothing about my religion besides the names of Hindu gods and goddesses and the Gayatri Mantra. Three lectures were devoted to Hinduism. Dr Ashby told us of the four Vedas, the Upanishads and the Bhagavad Gita. They made more sense to me than the other religious texts he had dealt with. 'Worship God in any form you like, that, essentially, is what Hinduism says,' explained Dr Ashby. 'Hindus have no prescribed scriptures: no Zend-Avesta, no Torah, no Bible, no Koran. Read what moves you the most. Seek the Truth within yourself.' And how spiritually elevating the message of the Gita was—Nish kama karma: do your duty without expectation of reward. When you engage in the battle of life, do so regardless of whether you win or lose, whether it gives you pleasure or pain. There was also the Lord's promise to come again and again to redeem the world from sin and evil-doing. Hinduism had no prophets, no one God, we were told. One could choose any deity one liked and worship him or her. By the end of that lecture I felt elated and wanted to shout: 'I am a Hindu and proud of being one.'

It was that woman in the front row who dampened my spirits. She launched into a furious monologue. 'Professor,' she began as soon as Dr Ashby had finished, 'what you said about Hindu philosophy is all very well. But tell us, why do the Hindus of today worship a monkey as a god, an elephant as a god; they worship trees, snakes, and rivers. They even worship the lingam, which is the phallus, and the yoni, the female genital, as god and goddess,' she screeched, thumping her desk. 'They have obscene sculptures on their temple walls. They have deities for measles, smallpox and plague. Their most popular god, Krishna, started out as a thief and lied when caught thieving; he stole girls' clothes while they were bathing so he could watch them naked; he had over one thousand mistresses; his lifelong companion was not his wife but his aunt Radha. Hinduism is the only religion in the world which declares a section of its followers outcastes by accident of birth. Hindus are the only people in the world who worship living humans as godmen and godwomen. I am told that there are nearly five hundred such men and women who claim to be bhagwans. They believe a dip in the Ganges washes away all their sins, so they can start sinning again! What basis is there for their belief that after death you are reborn in another form depending on your actions in this life? You may be reborn as a rat, mouse, cat, dog or a snake. *This* is what the Hindus of today believe in, not in the elevated teachings of the Vedas, Upanishads and the Gita! Should we not examine these aspects of Hinduism as practised today?'

There was stunned silence. The woman had spoken with such vehemence that there was little room left for objective dialogue. Dr Ashby restored the atmosphere to an academic level. 'This sort of thing could be said about all religions,' he said gently. 'What their founders taught and what their scriptures stand for are far removed from how they are interpreted and practised today. Our concern is with theory, not practice. Muslims condemn the worship of idols, yet they kiss the meteorite stone in the Kaaba and millions worship the graves of their saints.'

'I can explain Muslim practices,' replied the lady.

Before she could do so, however, the class was over.

'We will resume this discussion next week,' said Professor Ashby as he left the classroom.

I was fuming with rage. As the class began to disperse,

I quickly walked up to the woman and asked her, 'Madam, why do you hate Hindus so much?'

She was taken aback. 'I don't hate Hindus,' she protested. 'I don't hate anyone.' She looked me up and down as if she was seeing me for the first time. It had not occurred to her that I could be an Indian. She was contrite! 'Are you a Hindu from Bharat?' she asked.

'I am,' I replied as tersely as I could, 'and proud of being both. And I don't worship monkeys, elephants, snakes, phalluses or yonis. My religion is enshrined in one word, ahimsa, non-violence.'

She apologized. 'Please forgive me if I hurt your feelings. Perhaps one day you will enlighten me and clear the misgivings I have about Hindus and Bharat.' She put out her hand in a gesture of friendship. I shook it without much enthusiasm.

'My name is Yasmeen Wanchoo,' she said. 'I am from Azad Kashmir on a leadership grant.'

'I'm Mohan Kumar, from Delhi. I'm in business management and computer sciences.'

Like many Kashmiri women, Yasmeen was as fair-skinned as Caucasian women. She had nut-brown hair, large gazelle eyes and was fighting a losing battle with fat. She had a double chin, her arms had sagging flesh and there were tyres developing about her waist. She was, as the Punjabis say, goree chittee gole matole—fair, white and roly-poly. She was the first Pakistani woman I had ever spoken to, also the first Muslim. I wanted to know if there was any truth in the stories I had heard about Pakistanis hating Indians and the contempt Muslims had for Hindus. I hoped Yasmeen Wanchoo would tell me. It was not very long ago that our two countries had fought a war—their third—but I did not hate Pakistanis. Her outburst had shocked me. I have never understood hatred.

At the next class, she came up to me and said, 'No hard feelings. Come and sit next to me.' I declined. 'Madam, I sit in the last row, I hate being in the front.'

'In that case I'll sit with you in the last row. And do not "Madam" me, it makes me feel old. I am Yasmeen. And if you don't mind I'll call you Mohan.'

At the time, I had no steady date so I kept company with Yasmeen. She turned out to be not as aggressive as I had thought, and I began pulling her leg often about her being anti-Hindu and anti-Indian. She told me more about herself. 'My parents lived in Srinagar, now the capital of India-occupied Kashmir. Our forefathers were Brahmin Pandits till they had the good sense to convert to Islam. It is the best religion in the world. My parents lived in Srinagar till the Indian

Army occupied it, then they migrated to Muzaffarabad, the capital of Free Kashmir. I was born and educated there. I married another refugee from India, a Kashmiri, also of Brahmin descent—though Muslims, we don't marry below our caste. My husband is a minister in the Azad Kashmir Government. I am also active in politics and a member of the Assembly. We have three children.'

I asked her if she did not prefer the freedom she had in America to her life in Pakistan. She would not give me a straight answer. When I persisted, she got a little irritated and said, 'I love my family and my watan. We may not have succeeded yet, but one day we will liberate Kashmir from India's clutches and I will return to Srinagar which I have only seen in pictures.'

'And plant the Pakistani flag on Delhi's Red Fort,' I quipped.

'Inshallah!' she replied, beaming a smile at me.

'One day we will liberate your so-called Azad Kashmir from the clutches of Pakistan and make it a part of Indian Kashmir again.'

'You live in a fool's paradise,' she said, warming up. 'One Muslim warrior can take on ten of you Hindus.'

'So it was proved in the last war,' I replied sarcastically. 'The Pakistani army laid down arms after only thirteen days of fighting. Ninety-four thousand five hundred valiant Muslim warriors surrendered tamely to infidel Hindus and Sikhs without putting up a fight. In the history of the world there is no other instance of such abject surrender of an entire army.'

'Now you are being cruel,' she said, almost whining. 'You Indians are cheats. You misled those miserable Bengalis to rise against their Muslim brethren. Now they hate your guts and want to regain our friendship. You see what happens in the next Indo-Pak war.'

Despite our heated arguments, Yasmeen and I became friends. She could hardly be described as my date as she was almost twenty years older than me. She sought my company because there were not any men or women of her age on the campus. Though young, I was at least from her part of the world; she could talk to me in Hindustani. We often had coffee together. One day, out of the blue, she gave me a Gold Cross pen as a gift. I did not have much money to spare as I sent much of what I saved from my stipend, along with what I earned doing odd jobs in the library or working in the cafeteria, to my father. However, I started looking into shop windows to find something suitable as a return gift for Yasmeen.

After a couple of weeks, Professor Ashby went on to Islam. He gave us a long list of books to read—various histories of the Arabs, biographies of Prophet Mohammed, translations of the Koran, essays on Muslim sects and sub-sects. I did not bother to read any of them. What I looked forward to was Yasmeen's comments after the lectures. She did not disappoint me.

She kept her peace during the first two lectures in which Professor Ashby dealt with pre-Muslim Arabia, the life of the Prophet, revelations of the Koran, the Prophet's flight from Mecca to Medina, his victorious return to Mecca, the traditions ascribed to him, the speed at which his message spread to neighbouring countries, the Shia-Sunni schism and so on. It was factual information but not very inspiring. As soon as he had finished his second lecture, Yasmeen shot up from her seat beside me and delivered an impassioned harangue. 'What you have told us about Islam is historically accurate, Dr Ashby. What you haven't told us is why it is today the most vibrant of religions. This is because it is the most perfect of all religious systems with precise rules of dos and don'ts that everyone can follow. It was only to Prophet Mohammed (peace be upon Him) that God Himself sent down His message for mankind, Mohammed (peace be upon Him) was the most perfect human being that ever trod the face of the earth. There must be some reason behind the spectacular success of His mission. Within a few years of His death, Islam spread like wildfire from the Pacific Coast to the Atlantic Coast of Europe; it spread all over Asia and the African continent. It overcame the opposition of fire-worshippers, Jews, Christians, Buddhists and Hindus. Why does Islam gain more converts than any other religion? These are some of the questions that I would like the class to discuss.'

She sat down breathless after her speech. Only one student, a mild-mannered Jew who always wore a skullcap, took up her challenge. 'Perhaps the lady can answer some of my questions before I answer hers,' he said. 'Can she deny that Islam borrowed most of its ideas from Judaism? Their greeting, salam valaikum, is derived from the Hebrew shalom aleich; the names of their five daily prayers are taken from Judaism. We turn to Jerusalem to pray; they borrowed the idea from us, but instead, turn to Makka. Following the Jewish practice, they circumcise their male children. They have taken the concept of haraam (unlawful) and halaal (legitimate), what to eat and what not to eat, from the Jewish kosher. We Jews forbid eating pig's meat because we regard it as being unclean; Muslims do the same. We bleed animals to death before we eat them. Following us, so do they. They revere all the prophets revered by Jews and Christians. What was there in Islam which was very new? Everything it has is borrowed from Judaism or Christianity.'

Yasmeen was up on her feet again to do battle with the Jew. 'What was new was the advent of Prophet Mohammed (peace be upon Him). He was the greatest of all prophets sent by Allah, and any Muslim anywhere in the world knows this. We recognize no one after Mohammed (peace be upon Him).'

The Jew did not take that lying down. 'What about the division between Sunnis and Shias? Shias pay greater deference to the Prophet's cousin and son-in-law Ali than they do to the Prophet. And what about Muslim sects founded on sub-prophets of their own? The Aga Khans, Ismailies, Bohras, Ahmediyas and many others whose names I can't even remember? And while we are at it, I would like the lady to enlighten us on why, when Islam talks of giving a fair deal to women, it allows four wives to one man, why many Muslim rulers maintained large harems of women and eunuchs. Why are they forever calling for jehad—holy war—with infidels and fighting against each other?'

It was degenerating into a pointless wrangle. Professor Ashby put an end to it. 'I see we are in for another lively debate. Perhaps you can discuss these issues outside the class.'

The lecture period was over. Yasmeen's face was flushed with anger and triumph. 'Don't you think I put that miserable Jew in his place?' she asked me as we walked out. Instead of answering her question, I asked her, 'Yasmeen, why are you so kattar (bigoted)? Muslims are the most bigoted religious community in the world. Their Prophet was the greatest, their religion is the best, Muslims are the most enlightened community, the most God-fearing and righteous of all mankind. If the Jews think they are God's chosen people, Muslims think they are the choicest of the chosen. How can you be so narrow-minded?'

She was taken aback. 'We are not bigoted,' she retorted. 'We follow our religious precepts in letter and in spirit because we know they are the best for humanity. You must give me the opportunity to tell you of the beauty of Islam. You don't know what you are missing in life.'

'I'm happy in my ignorance,' I replied. 'I don't have much patience with any religion. All I say is try not to injure anyone's feelings. The rest is marginal. Gods, prophets, scriptures, rituals, pilgrimages mean very little to me.

She made no comment.

∽

Yasmeen had only a week left in Princeton. Having failed to find anything more suitable to give her, I bought her a University ring made of silver with the Princeton emblem on it. At a coffee session one morning, when no one was sharing our table, I took it out of my pocket and slipped it on her finger. 'I see you wear only gold but I could not afford a gold ring. And this being a University ring, no one will comment on it. You could have bought it yourself but I'm giving it to you so that it will remind you of your days with a Bharatiya Hindu boy in Princeton.'

She took my hand and kissed it. A faint blush came over her face. 'You are a nice boy. I only wish your name was not Mohan Kumar but Mohammed Kareem, or something like that,' she laughed. 'I am not as kattar as you think. I am just concerned about your future.'

During her last week in Princeton, we met every day. We spent the afternoons walking around the campus and shopping. She bought lots of things for her husband and children and her household in Muzaffarabad. She seemed to have plenty of cash and dollar traveller's cheques. Came her last day: she invited me over for dinner. 'Have you ever tasted Kashmiri food? It is the tastiest in the world, only very rich. I am a good cook. I can make very good goshtaba. Ever tasted goshtaba?'

I admitted that I had not.

'You must tell me what you don't eat,' she said. 'You Hindus have so many food fads. I know you don't eat beef or veal, but believe me, it is the most delicious meat. So many of you are vegetarian; no fish, not even eggs. Some even refuse to eat onions or garlic. How can you make anything tasty without onions or garlic, I ask you?'

'I eat everything except beef. Not that I regard the cow as sacred, but because I have been brought up like that. And let me assure you that pig's meat, which you will not touch, can be very clean and tasty: ham, bacon, pork are the staple diet of most Europeans and Americans. One reason why I don't think Islam will spread to the Pacific Islands is because their economy is based on the pig. And I know that like the Jews, many Muslims don't eat shrimps, crabs or lobsters. Muslim tribes living along the Arabian and African coast don't eat fish because they think fish are serpents of the sea.'

'You are a very argumentative fellow,' she said, patting my cheek. 'Come as early as you can tomorrow evening and sample my Kashmiri cooking. I don't drink, but I'll get some beer for you and put it in the fridge.'

I swear I had nothing more on my mind than spending a pleasant evening with Yasmeen. Things did not turn out that way. I took her a bunch of dark-red roses. She kissed my hands as I gave them to her and embraced me warmly. While I was casually dressed in a sports shirt and slacks, she wore a silk salwar-kameez with gold borders, a gold necklace with a medallion on which was inscribed a verse from the Koran, gold earrings and gold bangles. She had a lot of make-up on and had doused herself with French perfume. Besides beer in the fridge, she had put a half-bottle of Scotch, a tumbler and a pitcher of water on the centre table. 'You help yourself to Scotch or beer while I say my evening namaaz.'

She went to her bedroom, put her prayer mat on the floor and stood facing Mecca. I poured myself a Scotch. While I sipped it, I saw her going through her genuflections. She sat a long time on her knees with the palms of her hands open in front of her face as if reading their lines. I could see her lips moving but could not hear what she was reciting. She looked serene. She turned her face one way, then the other, brushed her face with her hands and stood up. She rolled up her prayer mat and tucked it under her bed.

She went into the kitchen to make sure the goshtaba was cooking nicely and lowered the flame so that it could cook slowly. Then she came and joined me. 'How's the drink?' she asked.

'Very nice,' I replied. 'Would you like one?'

'Toba! It is haraam. You will make me a sinner, will you? You can fetch me a Coke from the fridge.'

I got out a can of Coke. Before I could open it, she took it from my hand and put it on the table. Then she held my hands in hers and looked into my eyes till I had to lower my gaze, embarrassed. Suddenly, she put her arms round my neck and said, 'It is our last evening together. Make love to me—something to remember you by for the rest of my days.'

To say that I was shocked would be an understatement. This was the last thing I had expected of the evening. Besides, Yasmeen had never appeared sexually desirable to me. But she did not give me a chance to protest. She took me by my hand and led me to the bedroom. She took off everything save her jewellery. Her skin was soft but flabby. Her big breasts sagged and she had shaved her pubic hair. None of the girls I had bedded shaved their privates. I was surprised to find that a woman so large, who had borne three children, had such a small vagina. It looked vulnerable. While I gazed at her figure, she took off my shirt and pulled down my trousers. She gasped at what she saw. 'Mashallah! What have you got there? Do all Hindus have organs of this size? It must be their reward for worshipping the phallus.' She fondled it for a while with her pudgy hands, her lips glued to mine.

She pulled me over her and stretched her thighs wide to receive me. I entered her. She moaned with pleasure and locked her legs behind my back. She ate up my face with bites and passionate kisses. We came together.

She lay back exhausted. Then she pushed me off her and went into the bathroom to wash. She came back and put on her kameez. 'That goshtaba must be ready by now. It must not get overcooked. You wash yourself and I'll lay the dinner on the table.'

I did as I was told. She was like a political boss in full command of the situation. We sat down to eat. I noticed she had not put on her salwar. Her kameez hung down to her knees, exposing her broad thighs when she stood up or sat down. I understood that she had not finished with me and expected another session after dinner. I was not sure if I would be up to it with her. But I let myself in for it by a thoughtless gesture. While she was washing the dishes and I was drying them with a piece of cloth, I put my right hand under her kameez and stroked her huge buttocks. They were like two gourds of a tanpura joined together—massive, rounded, smooth. She smiled and kissed me on the lips. 'You want to do it a second time? So do I. We will make it different this time.' That did it.

For a while we sat holding hands and chatted away. She told me of her daily schedule in Muzaffarabad. 'With both my husband and I being in politics, we hardly have a moment to ourselves. It is like a public durbar from sunrise to sunset. Wherever we go we are surrounded by men and women with petitions. For me, being here is like being on a holiday. I wish I could extend it but my grant is over and my family will want to know why I am not taking the first flight back to Karachi and home.'

She stood up and stretched her arms above her head and stifled a yawn. 'Time for bed,' she said, taking me by the hand and leading me to her bed. She gently pushed me on it. 'This time you relax and I'll do all the work!'

She pulled off my trousers and fondled my limp lingam till it was ready for action. She sat astride my groin, spread her ample frame over me and directed my phallus into her. She was wet and eager and my penis slid in easily. Her breasts smothered my face. She held each in turn and put its nipple in my mouth, urging me to suck it. She kissed me hungrily and noisily on my nose, lips and neck, leaving her saliva on me, while she heaved and thumped me with her huge buttocks. 'I haven't had sex for six months. I am famished,' she said as her movements became more frenzied. 'Fill me up with all you have, you miserable kafir,' she screamed. And with a spectacular shudder and a loud ha, ha, ha she collapsed on me like a lifeless corpse. She did all the fucking. I was simply fucked.

'Wouldn't it be nicer if we settled Pak-India problems this way rather than by abusing each other and fighting?' she asked after a while.

'Sure,' I replied. 'And with Pakistan always on top?'

'Of course! Pakistan must always be on top.'

I was exhausted, and wanted to get away.

She clung to me and begged, 'Please stay the night with me. I'll feel very lost if you go away. I promise I won't bother you anymore.'

I agreed to spend the night with her and see her off at the bus stand the next morning. I could not resist asking her a few awkward questions. 'You must tell me how you square your belief in Islamic values with what you and I have been doing.'

She paused a long time, fixed me with her large eyes. 'What I did was sinful,' she admitted.

'A sin punishable with death by stoning?'

She was quiet for a long time.

'Doesn't your conscience bother you?' I asked.

'The body has its compulsions,' she said.

'I'm sure it has, but that's the easy way to square your conscience.'

'What would you have me do?'

'I have no idea. But surely there must be something in your religion that allows you to absolve yourself of your sins by going on a pilgrimage?'

'I suppose so,' she said evasively.

'Like the Hindus being forgiven if they take a dip in the Holy Ganga?' I teased.

'Oh shut up!' she shouted angrily. 'Don't spoil my last night with you.'

She put her head on my right arm and nestled against me. 'You are more curious about things than is good for you.'

'What do you mean?'

'You know, all those questions about my religion and my conscience.'

I laughed and pulled her close and kissed her passionately.

We were soon fast asleep in each other's arms.

NOORAN

∽

Juggut Singh had been gone from his home about an hour. He had only left when the sound of the night goods train told him that it would now be safe to go. For him, as for the dacoits, the arrival of the train that night was a signal. At the first distant rumble, he slipped quietly off his charpoy and picked up his turban and wrapped it round his head. Then he tiptoed across the courtyard to the haystack and fished out a spear. He tiptoed back to his bed, picked up his shoes, and crept towards the door.

'Where are you going?'

Juggut Singh stopped. It was his mother. 'To the fields,' he said. 'Last night, wild pigs did a lot of damage.'

'Pigs!' his mother said. 'Don't try to be clever. Have

you forgotten already that you are on probation—that it is forbidden for you to leave the village after sunset? And with a spear! Enemies will see you. They will report you. They will send you back to jail.' Her voice rose to a wail. 'Then who will look after the crops and the cattle?'

'I will be back soon,' Juggut Singh said. 'There is nothing to worry about. Everyone in the village is asleep.'

'No,' his mother said. She wailed again.

'Shut up,' he said. 'It is you who will wake the neighbours. Be quiet and there will be no trouble.'

'Go! Go wherever you want to go. If you want to jump in a well, jump. If you want to hang like your father, go and hang. It is my lot to weep. My kismet,' she added, slapping her forehead, 'it is all written there.'

Juggut Singh opened the door and looked on both sides. There was no one about. He walked along the walls till he got to the end of the lane near the pond. He could see the grey forms of a couple of adjutant storks slowly pacing up and down in the mud looking for frogs. They paused in their search. Juggut Singh stood still against the wall till the storks were reassured, then went off the footpath across the fields towards the river. He crossed the dry sand bed till he got to the stream. He stuck his spear in the ground with the blade pointing upward, then stretched out on the sand. He lay on his back and gazed at the stars. A meteor shot across the Milky Way, trailing a silver path across the blue-black sky. Suddenly, a hand was placed on his eyes. 'Guess who?'

Juggut Singh stretched out his hands over his head and behind him, groping; the girl dodged them. Starting with the hand on his eyes, Juggut Singh felt his way up from the arm to the shoulder and then on to the face. He caressed the girl's cheeks, eyes and nose that his hands knew so well. He tried to play with her lips to induce them to kiss his fingers. The girl opened her mouth and bit him fiercely. Juggut Singh jerked his hand away. With a quick movement he caught the girl's head in both his hands and brought her face over to his. Then he slipped his arms under her waist and hoisted her into the air above him with her arms and legs kicking about like a crab. He turned her about till his arms ached. He brought her down flat upon him limb to limb.

The girl slapped him on the face.

'You put your hands on the person of a strange woman! Have you not mother or sister in your home? Have you no shame? No wonder the police have got you on their register as a bad character. I will also tell the Inspector Sahib that you are a budmash.'

'I am only a budmash with you, Nooro. We should both be locked up in the same cell.'

'You have learned to talk too much. I will have to look for another man.'

Juggut Singh crossed his arms behind the girl's back and crushed her till she could not talk or breathe. Every time she started to speak he tightened his arms round her and her words got stuck in her throat. She gave up and put her exhausted face against his. He laid her beside him with her head nestling in the hollow of his left arm. With his right hand he stroked her hair and face.

The goods train engine whistled twice and with a lot of groaning and creaking began to puff its way towards the bridge. The storks flew up from the pond with shrill cries and came towards the river. From the river they flew back to the pond, calling alternately, long after the train had gone over the bridge and its puff-puffs had died into silence.

Juggut Singh's caresses became lustful.

His hand strayed from the girl's face to her breasts and her waist. She caught it and put it back on her face. His breathing became slow and sensuous. His hand wandered again and brushed against her breasts as if by mistake. The girl slapped it and put it away. Juggut

Singh stretched his left arm that lay under the girl's head and caught her reproving hand. Her other arm was already under him. She was defenceless.

'No! No! No! Let go of my hand! No! I will never speak to you again.' She shook her head violently from side to side, trying to avoid his hungry mouth.

Juggut Singh slipped his hand inside her shirt and felt the contours of her unguarded breasts. They became taut. The nipples became hard and leathery. His rough hands gently moved from her breasts to her navel. The skin on her belly came up in goose flesh.

The girl continued to wriggle and protest. 'No! No! No! Please! May Allah's curse fall on you! Let go of my hand. I will never meet you again if you behave like this.' Juggut Singh's searching hand found one end of the cord of her trousers. He pulled it with a jerk.

'No,' cried the girl hoarsely.

A shot rang through the night. The storks flew up from the pond calling to each other.

Crows started cawing in the keekar trees. Juggut Singh paused and looked up into the darkness towards the village. The girl quietly extricated herself from his hold and adjusted her dress. The crows settled back on the trees. The storks flew away across the river. Only the dogs barked.

'It sounded like a gunshot,' she said nervously, trying to keep Juggut Singh from renewing his lovemaking. 'Wasn't it from the village?'

'I don't know. Why are you trying to run away? It is all quiet now.' Juggut Singh pulled her down beside him.

'This is no time for jesting. There is murder in the village. My father will get up and want to know where I have gone. I must get back at once.'

'No, you will not. I won't let you. You can say you were with a girl friend.'

'Don't talk like a stupid peasant. How...' Juggut Singh shut her mouth with his. He bore upon her with his enormous weight. Before she could free her arms he ripped open the cord of her trousers once again.

'Let me go. Let me...'

She could not struggle against Juggut Singh's brute force. She did not particularly want to. Her world was narrowed to the rhythmic sound of breathing and the warm smell of dusky skins raised to fever heat. His lips slobbered over her eyes and cheeks. His tongue sought the insides of her ears. In a state of frenzy she dug her nails into his thinly bearded cheeks and bit his nose. The stars above her went into a mad whirl and then came back to their places like a merry-go-round slowly coming to a stop. Life came back to its cooler, lower level. She felt the dead weight of the lifeless man, the sand grits in her hair, the breeze trespassing on her naked limbs, the censorious stare of the myriad of stars. She pushed Juggut Singh away. He lay down beside her.

'That is all you want. And you get it. You are just a peasant. Always wanting to sow your seed. Even if the world were going to hell you would want to do that. Even when guns are being fired in the village. Wouldn't you?' she nagged.

'Nobody is firing any guns. Just your imagination,' answered Juggut Singh wearily, without looking at her.

Faint cries of wailing wafted across to the riverside. The couple sat up to listen. Two shots rang out in quick succession. The crows flew out of the keekars, cawing furiously.

The girl began to cry.

'Something is happening in the village. My father will wake up and know I have gone out. He will kill me.' Juggut Singh was not listening to her. He did not know what to do. If his absence from the village was discovered, he would be in trouble with the police. That did not bother him as much as the trouble the girl would be in. She might not come again. She was saying so: 'I will never come to see you again. If Allah forgives me this time, I will never do it again.'

'Will you shut up or do I have to smack your face?'

The girl began to sob. She found it hard to believe this was the same man who had been making love to her a moment ago. 'Quiet! There is someone coming,' whispered Juggut Singh, putting his heavy hand over her mouth.

The couple lay still, peering into the dark. Five men carrying guns and spears passed within a few yards of them. They had uncovered their faces and were talking. 'Dakoo! Do you know them?' the girl asked in a whisper.

'Yes,' Juggut said, 'the one with the torch is Malli.' His face went tight. 'That incestuous lover of his sister! I've told him a thousand times this is no time for dacoities. And now he has brought his gang to my village! I will settle this with him.'

The dacoits went up to the river and then downstream towards the ford a couple of miles to the south. A pair of lapwings pierced the still night with startled cries: 'Teet-titteetittee-whoot, tee-tee-whoot, tee-tee-whoot, tittittee-whoot.'

'Will you report them to the police?' Juggut Singh sniggered. 'Let us get back before they miss me in the village.'

The pair walked back towards Mano Majra, the man in front, the girl a few paces behind him. They could hear the sound of wailing and the barking of dogs. Women were shouting to each other across the roofs. The whole village seemed to be awake. Juggut Singh stopped near the pond and turned around to speak to the girl.

'Nooro, will you come tomorrow?' he asked, pleading.

'You think of tomorrow and I am bothered about my life. You have your good time even when I am murdered.'

'No one can harm you while I live. No one in Mano Majra can raise his eyebrows at you and get away from Jugga. I am not a budmash for nothing,' said he haughtily. 'You tell me tomorrow what happens or the day after tomorrow when all this—whatever it is—is over. After the goods train?'

'No! No! No!' answered the girl. 'What will I say to my father now? This noise is bound to have woken him.'

'Just say you had gone out. Your stomach was upset or something like that. You heard the firing and were hiding till the dacoits had left. Will you come the day after tomorrow then?'

'No,' she repeated, this time a little less emphatically. The excuse might work. Just as well her father was almost blind. He would not see her silk shirt, nor the antimony in her eyes. Nooran walked away into the darkness, swearing she would never come again.

Juggut Singh went up the lane to his house. The door was open. Several villagers were in the courtyard talking to his mother. He turned around quietly and made his way back to the river.

∽

Before going round to other Muslim homes, Imam Baksh went to his own hut attached to the mosque. Nooran was already in bed. An oil lamp burned in a niche in the wall.

'Nooro, Nooro,' he shouted, shaking her by the shoulder. 'Get up, Nooro.'

The girl opened her eyes. 'What is the matter?'

'Get up and pack. We have to go away tomorrow morning,' he announced dramatically.

'Go away? Where?'

'I don't know...Pakistan!'

The girl sat up with a jerk. 'I will not go to Pakistan,' she said defiantly.

Imam Baksh pretended he had not heard. 'Put all the clothes in the trunks and the cooking utensils in a gunny bag. Also take something for the buffalo. We will have to take her too.'

'I will not go to Pakistan,' the girl repeated, fiercely.

'You may not want to go, but they will throw you out. All Muslims are leaving for the camp tomorrow.'

'Who will throw us out? This is our village. Are the police and the government dead?'

'Don't be silly, girl. Do as you are told. Hundreds of thousands of people are going to Pakistan and as many coming out. Those who stay behind are killed. Hurry up and pack. I have to go and tell the others that they must get ready.'

Imam Baksh left the girl sitting up in bed. Nooran rubbed her face with her hands and stared at the wall. She did not know what to do. She could spend the night out and come back when all the others had gone. But she could not do it alone; and it was raining. Her only chance was Jugga. Malli had been released, maybe Jugga had also come home. She knew that was not true, but the hope persisted and it gave her something to do.

Nooran went out in the rain. She passed many people in the lanes, going about with gunny bags covering their heads and shoulders. The whole village was awake. In most houses she could see the dim flickers of oil lamps. Some were packing; others were helping them to pack. Most just talked with their friends. The women sat on the floors hugging each other and crying. It was as though there had been a death in every home.

Nooran shook the door of Jugga's house.

The chain on the other side rattled but there was no response. In the grey light she noticed the door was bolted from the outside. She undid the iron ring and went in. Jugga's mother was out, probably visiting some Muslim friends. There was no light at all. Nooran sat down on a charpoy. She did not want to face Jugga's mother alone nor did she want to go back home. She hoped something would happen—something that would make Jugga walk in. She sat and waited and hoped.

For an hour Nooran watched the grey shadows of clouds chasing each other. It drizzled and poured and poured and drizzled alternately. She heard the sound of footsteps cautiously picking their way through the muddy lane. They stopped outside the door. Someone shook the door.

'Who is it?' asked an old woman's voice. Nooran lost her nerve; she did not move. 'Who is it?' demanded the voice angrily. 'Why don't you speak?'

Nooran stood up and mumbled indistinctly, 'Beybey.'

The old woman stepped in and quickly shut the door behind her.

'Jugga! Jugga, is it you?' she whispered. 'Have they let you off?'

'No, Beybey, it is I, Nooran, Chacha Imam Baksh's daughter,' answered the girl timidly.

'Nooro? What brings you here at this hour?' the old woman asked angrily.

'Has Jugga come back?'

'What have you to do with Jugga?' his mother snapped. 'You have sent him to jail. You have made him a budmash. Does your father know you go visiting strangers' houses at midnight like a tart?'

Nooran began to cry. 'We are going away tomorrow.'

That did not soften the old woman's heart.

'What relation are you to us that you want to come to see us? You can go where you like.'

Nooran played her last card. 'I cannot leave. Jugga has promised to marry me.'

'Get out, you bitch!' the old woman hissed. 'You, a Muslim weaver's daughter, marry a Sikh peasant! Get out, or I will go and tell your father and the whole village. Go to Pakistan! Leave my Jugga alone.'

Nooran felt heavy and lifeless. 'All right, Beybey, I will go. Don't be angry with me. When Jugga comes back just tell him I came to say "Sat Sri Akal."' The girl went down on her knees, clasped the old woman's legs and began to sob. 'Beybey, I am going away and will never come back again. Don't be harsh to me just when I am leaving.'

Jugga's mother stood stiff, without a trace of emotion

on her face. Inside, she felt a little weak and soft. 'I will tell Jugga.'

Nooran stopped crying. Her sobs came at long intervals. She still held on to Jugga's mother. Her head sank lower and lower till it touched the old woman's feet.

'Beybey.'

'What have you to say now?' She had a premonition of what was coming.

'Beybey.'

'Beybey! Beybey! Why don't you say something?' asked the woman, pushing Nooran away. 'What is it?'

The girl swallowed the spittle in her mouth.

'Beybey, I have Jugga's child inside me. If I go to Pakistan they will kill it when they know it has a Sikh father.'

The old woman let Nooran's head drop back on her feet. Nooran clutched them hard and began to cry again.

'How long have you had it?'

'I have just found out. It is the second month.'

Jugga's mother helped Nooran up and the two sat down on the charpoy. Nooran stopped sobbing.

'I cannot keep you here,' said the old woman at last. 'I have enough trouble with the police already. When all this is over and Jugga comes back, he will go and get you from wherever you are. Does your father know?'

'No! If he finds out he will marry me off to someone or murder me.' She started crying again.

'Oh, stop this whining,' commanded the old woman sternly. 'Why didn't you think of it when you were at the mischief? I have already told you, Jugga will get you as soon as he is out.'

Nooran stifled her sobs.

'Beybey, don't let him be too long.'

'He will hurry for his own sake. If he does not get you he will have to buy a wife and there is not a pice or trinket left with us. He will get you if he wants a wife. Have no fear.'

A vague hope filled Nooran's being. She felt as if she belonged to the house and the house to her; the charpoy she sat on, the buffalo, Jugga's mother, all were hers. She could come back even if Jugga failed to turn up. She could tell them she was married. The thought of her father came like a dark cloud over her lunar hopes. She would slip away without telling him. The moon shone again.

'Beybey, if I get the chance I will come to say Sat Sri Akal in the morning. Sat Sri Akal. I must go and pack now.' Nooran hugged the old woman passionately. 'Sat

Sri Akal,' she said a little breathlessly again and went out.

Jugga's mother sat on her charpoy staring into the dark for several hours.

THE VENUS OF CHURCHGATE

❦

For the first few months after taking over the editorship of *The Illustrated Weekly of India*, I lived as a paying guest of a young Parsi couple in a flat in Churchgate. I did not know many people, so had very little of a social life. I walked to the office every morning and walked back every evening as I refused to use the car and chauffeur provided for me.

Among the earliest friends I made was A.G. Noorani who combined practising law with journalism. He was, and is, a bachelor. We began to spend our evenings together. We would go for a stroll along Marine Drive and return to my flat.

I had my evening ration of Scotch; Noorani, who was and is a teetotaller, had a glass of aerated water.

Then we set off to try out different restaurants in the neighbourhood. After dinner we tried different paanwalas and bade each other good night. This routine was upset with the onset of the monsoon in Bombay. That's when I ran into the lady about whom I write.

There was a break in the downpour. I was alone as I stepped out of a restaurant. A gas station and a few shops were on my way home. I stopped there to buy myself a paan and chatted with a bhelpuriwala and asked him how his business was during the rains. 'Not very well,' he admitted. 'Magar iski kismat jaag jatee hai (her fortune increases),' he added pointing to a woman sitting on the steps of a shop nearby. 'What I can't sell, I give to her. She is a beggar. Thori paagal hai (she is a little mad).' I looked at the woman devouring bhelpuri.

An uncommonly attractive girl, she was in her mid-twenties. Fair, beautifully proportioned, uncombed hair wildly scattered about her face, a dirty white dhoti untidily draped around her body. I gazed at her for quite some time and wondered what an attractive young woman was doing alone in this vice-ridden city. I fantasized about her long into the night.

Thereafter, I made it a point to buy my after-dinner paan from the same paanwala by the gas station, exchange a few words with the bhelpuriwala as I ogled at the beggar maid on the steps of the closed shop. I often saw her talking to herself. I tried to buy bhelpuri to give to the girl, but the stall owner rejected my offer. He had plenty of leftovers, and feeding the girl was his monopoly.

One evening while I was at dinner, the clouds burst in all their fury and the roads around Churchgate were flooded. I tucked my trousers up to my knees, took my sandals in my hands, unfurled my umbrella to save my turban and waded through the swirling muddy water. Both the paanwala and the bhelpuriwala had shut shop and gone home. I saw the beggar girl stretched out on the marble steps barely an inch above the stream of rain water running past her. She couldn't have had anything to eat that night. I was sorely tempted to give her some money but was not sure how she would react. I walked home thinking about her, and again thought about her late into the night.

It poured all through the night. As I woke up to look out of the window that overlooked the maidan with the Rajabhai clock tower on the other side, the rain was still coming down in sheets. The maidan was flooded. I saw the shadowy figure of a woman walking across the maidan with a tin in her hand. I saw her hike her wet dhoti and start splashing water between her buttocks. I trained my field glasses on her. She turned to see whether anyone was around. Having reassured herself that she wasn't being watched, she took off her dhoti and stood stark naked in the pouring rain. It was my beggar woman. She poured dirty water on her body, rubbed her bosom, waist, arms and legs. The 'bath' over, she put the wet dhoti back on her and sloshed her way back towards Churchgate station.

The vision of Venus arising out of the sea in the form of a beggar maid of Bombay haunted me for the many days that I was away in Delhi. When I returned to Bombay I made it a point to go to Churchgate for my after-dinner stroll. The paanwala and the bhelpuriwala were there. But not the beggar. I asked the bhelpuriwala what had happened to the girl. His eyes filled with tears and his voice choked as he replied: 'Saaley bharwey utha ke lay gaye (the bloody pimps abducted her).'

MY WIFE, KAVAL

⚘

Most people who don't know me or my family are under the impression that my wife doesn't exist or that she is tucked away in some village like the wives of many of our netas. This is a grievous error, as my wife is quite a formidable character who rules the home with as firm a hand as Indira Gandhi ruled India. Unlike the mod girls of today who bob their hair, wear T-shirts, jeans and speak chi chi Hinglish, but when it comes to being married, tamely surrender their right to choose husbands to their parents, my wife made her own choice over sixty years ago.

I soon learnt that I could not take my wife for granted. If she did not like any of my friends, she told them so to their faces and in no uncertain terms. She is a stronger woman than any I have known. Her mother was very upset when she discovered that she drank whisky. One evening her mother stormed into the room, picked up her glass and threw it on the marble floor. The glass did not break bur slithered across the floor, spilling its contents. My wife quickly picked it up and refilled it. 'I am an adult and a married woman. You have no right to dictate to me,' she told her mother. When her mother was suffering from cancer, she asked her to promise that she would say her prayers regularly. Despite my pleas to say 'yes' to her dying mother, she refused to do so. 'I will not make a promise that I know I will not keep.' She nursed her mother for many months, sitting with her head in her lap and pressing it all through the nights. She was with her when she died. She took her bath and went to the coffee house to have her breakfast. When some friends asked her about her mother's health she replied, 'She is okay.' She then came home and told the servants that she would not receive any visitors who came to condole with her. She did not shed a tear. She did not go to her mother's funeral or any of the religious ceremonies that followed. On the other hand, when our dog Simba fell ill, she sat all night stroking him. When he died at the ripe old age of fourteen, she was heartbroken.

The rigid discipline of time maintained in our home is entirely due to my wife. I have only recently taught myself how to speed the departure of long-winded visitors. She has always given short shrift to them. No one drops in on us without prior warning. If any relation breezes in in the morning, she ignores his or her presence and continues with her housework and decides the menus for the day. (We eat the most gourmet meals; French, Chinese, Italian, South Indian and occasionally Punjabi. She has two shelves full of cookery books which she consults before discussing the meals with our cook Chandan, who has been with us for over thirty years.) Or she continues to teach the servants' children and help them with their homework. We don't accept lunch or tea invitations nor offer them. When we have people over for dinner, no matter who they are, whether Cabinet ministers or ambassadors, they are reminded to be punctual and told that we do not expect our guests to stay after 9 p.m. Once the German ambassador and his wife had come over. The meal was finished at 8.30 p.m. Liqueurs were served. It was 8.45 p.m. The Ambassador took out his cigar and asked my wife, 'I know, Mrs Singh, that you like your guests to leave before 9 p.m., but can I have my cigar before we go?' My wife promptly replied, 'I am sure, Mr

Ambassador, you will enjoy it more in your car.' He laughed and stood up saying, 'I get it.' And departed without any rancour.

A lot of pretty girls visit me. They are dead scared of my wife and know that they have to be on her right side to keep dropping in. All of them take good care never to offend her.

Why do so few people know about my wife? She is allergic to photographers and pressmen. All you have to do is take out your camera, tape recorder or pen and she will order you out of the house. The allergy runs in the women in the family. My daughter and granddaughter react the same way.

∽

It was during my stay in Welwyn Garden in my first year in England, that I ran into a girl, Kaval Malik, who had been with me at Modern School. She had always been a good-looking, light-skinned girl and a bit of a tomboy, playing hockey and soccer with the boys. When I left school, she was still a gawky girl, a couple of years my junior. I had lost track of her when I moved to Lahore. When I ran into her in England, she had blossomed into a beauty and was much sought after by many boys I knew, some from India's richest families. Her parents were orthodox Sikhs and were determined to marry her off to a Sikh boy in the Civil Services. They stood in awe of the Indian Civil Service, and her uncle, who had made it, was worshipped as a hero. At the time, they were negotiating with parents of Sikh boys sitting for competitive exams. Meeting the girl now grown into a young lady caused me anguish, as I fell desperately in love with her and also felt that I stood little chance of winning her. Amongst other obstacles was the fact that her father was a senior engineer in the Public Works Department (PWD), while mine was a builder who had to get contracts from the same. Besides, I was studying law, and lawyers, being a dime a dozen, were poorly rated in the marriage market. Her parents thought well of me, as a year earlier they had visited me in my lodgings. Her mother had found the Sikh prayer book under my pillow and had been deeply impressed. I met them again in the Lake District. They were staying in a fancy hotel at Bowness; I, in a lodging house at Windermere. I rowed up seven miles to have breakfast with them. I knew they would agree to their daughter marrying me if they could not find a better Sikh proposal.

My best chance was to bypass the parents and approach the girl directly. The Christmas vacations were near and she had nowhere to go. I suggested that she come with me to the Quaker hostel in Buckinghamshire. She wrote to her parents to seek their permission. To my utter surprise, they agreed that she could go. I began courting her as soon as the train left London. And continued paying court throughout our fortnight's stay with the Quakers. On our way back to London, I asked her if I could ask my parents to approach hers with the proposal. She nodded her consent.

Our engagement was announced a few days later. It caused a lot of heartache amongst her many suitors. A particularly ardent one, whose sister was married to my fiancée's brother, said very acidly, 'The bank balance won.' By that time, my father was known to be a man of considerable wealth. Though most of them envied me, the only one to try to dissuade me from marrying the girl was my closest friend, E.N. Mangat Rai, who, at the time, had a poor opinion of her. He later fell deeply in love with her and almost succeeded in wrecking our marriage.

It took me a year more than prescribed to take my bachelor of law degree, and I became a Barrister-at-Law of the Inner Temple. In the meantime, I had sat for the Indian Civil Service exam. Rating my chances as negligible, I had not taken one paper. When the results were declared, I discovered to my great surprise that I had just missed getting in. I was the only candidate, English or Indian, to be given full marks in the viva voce. I must have impressed the interview board more than the examiners of my papers.

I returned home by sea in the summer of 1939. There was talk of war breaking out. By the time I reached Delhi, German armies had been launched on their conquest of neighbouring countries.

In October 1939, I got married. It was a grand affair. My wife's father was by then chief engineer of the PWD, the first Indian to rise to the position. My father was acknowledged as the biggest owner of real estate in Delhi. We lived in a large stone-and-marble mansion with over a dozen bedrooms, a teak-panelled library, and chandeliered living and dining rooms. At our wedding reception there were over fifteen hundred guests, including M.A. Jinnah, founding father of Pakistan. Champagne flowed like the Jamuna in flood. My wife received presents which, even after fifty years of being given away, were not exhausted. My father gave me a new car and rented an apartment and office space for me near the High Court in Lahore. And after a short honeymoon at Mount Abu in Rajasthan, the two of us drove to Lahore in our new Ford.

PHOOLAN DEVI

❧

It was the afternoon of Saturday, 14 February 1981. Winter had given way to spring. Amidst the undulating sea of ripening wheat and green lentil were patches of bright yellow mustard in flower. Skylarks rose from the ground, suspended themselves in the blue skies and poured down song on the earth below. Allah was in His heaven and all was peace and tranquillity in Behmai.

Behmai is a tiny hamlet along the river Jamuna inhabited by about fifty families belonging mainly to the Thakur caste, with a sprinkling of shepherds and ironsmiths. Although it is only eighty miles from the industrial metropolis, Kanpur, it has no road connecting it to any town. To get to Behmai you have to traverse dusty footpaths meandering through cultivated fields, and go down narrow, snake-infested ravines choked with camel thorn and elephant grass. It is not surprising that till the middle of February, few people had heard of Behmai. After what happened on Saturday the 14th, it was on everyone's lips.

There was not much to do in the fields except drive off wild pigs and deer. Some boys armed with catapults and loud voices were out doing this; others played on the sand bank while their buffaloes wallowed in the mud. Men dozed on their charpoys; women sat in huddles gossiping as they ground corn or picked lice out of their children's hair.

No one in Behmai noticed a party dressed in police uniforms cross the river. It was led by a young woman with cropped hair wearing the khaki coat of a deputy superintendent of police with three silver stars, blue jeans and boots with zippers. She wore lipstick and her nails had varnish on them. Her belt was charged with bullets and had a curved Gurkha knife—a khukuri—attached to it. A Sten gun was slung across her shoulders and she carried a battery-fitted megaphone in her hand. The party sat down beside the village shrine adorned with the trident emblem of Shiva, the God of destruction.

The eldest of the party, a notorious gangster named

Baba Mustaqeem, instructed the group on how to go about their job: A dozen men were to surround the village so that no one could get out; the remaining men, led by the woman, were to search all the houses and take whatever they liked. But no women were to be raped nor anyone except the two men they were looking for, to be slain. They listened in silence and nodded their heads in agreement. They touched the base of Shiva's trident for good luck and dispersed.

The girl in the officer's uniform went up on the parapet of the village well, switched on the megaphone and shouted at the top of her voice, 'Listen you fellows! You bhosreekey (progenies of the cunt)! If you love your lives, hand over all the cash, silver and gold you have. And listen again! I know those madarchods (motherfuckers) Lal Ram Singh and Shri Ram Singh are hiding in this village. If you don't hand them over to me I will stick my gun into your bums and tear them apart. You've heard me. This is Phoolan Devi speaking. If you don't get cracking, you know what Phoolan Devi will do to you. Jai Durga Mata (Victory to the Mother Goddess, Durga)!' She raised her gun and fired a single shot in the air to convince them that she meant what she said.

Phoolan Devi stayed at the well while her men went

looting the Thakurs' homes. Women were stripped of their earrings, nose pins, silver bangles and anklets. Men handed over whatever cash they had on their persons. The operation lasted almost an hour. But there was no trace of Lal Ram Singh or Shri Ram Singh. The people of the village denied ever having seen them. 'You are lying!' roared Phoolan Devi. 'I will teach you to tell the truth.' She ordered all the young men to be brought before her. About thirty were dragged out to face her. She asked them again, 'You motherfuckers, unless you tell me where those two sons of pigs are, I will roast you alive.' The men pleaded with her and swore they had never seen the two men.

'Take these fellows along,' she ordered her men. 'I'll teach them a lesson they will never forget.' The gang pushed the thirty villagers out of Behmai along the path leading to the river. At an embankment, she ordered them to be halted and lined up. 'For the last time, will you tell me where those two bastards are, or do I have to kill you?' she asked, pointing her Sten gun at them. The villagers again pleaded ignorance. 'If we knew, we would tell you.'

'Turn round,' thundered Phoolan Devi. The men turned their faces towards the green embankment. 'Bhosreekey, this will also teach you not to report to the police. Shoot the bloody bastards!' she ordered her men and yelled, 'Jai Durga Mata!' There was a burst of gunfire. The thirty men crumpled to the earth. Twenty died; the others, hit in their limbs or buttocks, lay sprawled in blood-spattered dust.

Phoolan Devi and her murderous gang went down the path yelling, 'Jai Durga Mata! Jai Baba Mustaqeem! Jai Bikram Singh! Jai Phoolan Devi!'

The next morning, the massacre of Behmai made front-page headlines in all newspapers all over India.

Dacoity in India is as old as history. In some regions it is endemic and no sooner are some gangs liquidated than others come up. The most notorious dacoit country is a couple of hundred miles south-west of Behmai, along the ravines of the Chambal river in Madhya Pradesh. In the Bundelkhand district of Uttar Pradesh in which Behmai is located, it is of comparatively recent origin and the state police suspect that when things became too hot around the Chambal, some gangs migrated to Bundelkhand where the terrain was very much like the one they were familiar with. The river Jamuna, after its descent from the Himalayas, runs a sluggish, serpentine course past Delhi and Agra into Bundelkhand. Here it passes through a range of low-lying hills covered with dense forests. Several monsoon, fed rivulets running through deep gorges join it as it goes on to meet the holy Ganga at Allahabad. It is wild and beautiful country: hills, ravines and forests enclosing small picturesque hamlets. By day there are peacocks and multicoloured butterflies; by night, night jars calling to each other across the pitch-black wilderness flecked by fireflies. Nilgai, spotted deer, wild boar, hyena, jackal and fox abound. It is also infested with snakes, the commonest being cobras, the most venomous of the species. Cultivation is sparse and entirely dependent on rain. The chief produce are lentils and wheat. The peasantry is amongst the poorest in the country. The two main communities living along the river banks are Mallahs (boatmen) and Thakurs. The Thakurs are the higher caste and own most of the land. The Mallahs are amongst the lowest in the Hindu caste hierarchy, own little land and live mostly by plying boats, fishing and distilling liquor. Till recently, dacoit gangs were mixed: Thakurs, Mallahs, Yadavs (cattlemen), Gujjars (milkmen) and Muslims. But now, more and more are tending to becoming caste-oriented. There is little love lost between the Thakurs and the Mallahs. Behmai is a Thakur village; Phoolan Devi, a Mallahin.

No stigma is attached to being a dacoit; in their own territory they are known as bagis or rebels. Hindi movies, notably the biggest box-office hit of all time, *Sholay*, in which the hero is a dacoit, has added romance to the profession of banditry.

Dacoit gangs are well-equipped with automatic weapons, including self-loading rifles acquired mostly through raids. A police note on anti-dacoity operations records that Jalaun district which includes Behmai, has fifteen gangs of between ten to thirty members each operating in the area. Phoolan Devi and her current paramour, Man Singh Yadav, have fifteen men with them. In the last six months, the police have had ninety-three encounters with dacoits in which they killed 159 and captured 137. Forty-seven surrendered themselves, still roam about the jungles and ravines, hunting and being hunted.

❦

I sat on the parapet of the village well, on the same spot from where Phoolan Devi had announced her arrival in Behmai a year and a half earlier. In front of me sat village men, women and children and the police escort provided for me. An old woman wailed, 'That Mallahin killed my husband and two sons. May she die a dog's death!' A man stood up and bared his belly which showed gun-shot scars. Another bared his buttocks and pointed to a dimple where a bullet had hit him.

'Can any of you tell me why Phoolan Devi came to this village and killed so many people?' I asked.

No one answered.

'Is it true that Lal Ram Singh and Shri Ram Singh were in Behmai?' A chorus of voices answered: 'No, we have never seen them.'

'Is it true that a few months before the dacoity they had brought Phoolan Devi with them, raped her for several weeks before she managed to escape?'

'Ram! Ram! protested some of them, 'We had never seen the Mallahin in this village before the dacoity.'

'Why then, did she ask for the two brothers? How did she know her way about this village?'

No one answered.

'You will not get anything out of these fellows,' the police inspector said to me in English. 'You know what these villagers are! They never tell the truth.'

I gave up my cross-examination and decided to go around Behmai. I started from the village shrine with the Shiva's trident, came back to the well and then to the embankment where she had killed the twenty men. I went up a mound where the police had set up a sentry box from which I could get a bird's-eye view of the village, the Jamuna and the country beyond. The police sentinel on duty who had been in the village for several weeks volunteered the following information: 'Sir, I think I can tell you why Phoolan Devi did what she did. You see that village across the Jamuna on top of the hill? It is called Pal, it is a Mallah village. Mallahs used to come through Behmai to take the ferry. Thakur boys used to tease their girls and beat up their men. I am told there were several instances when they stripped the girls naked and forced them to dance. The Mallahs appealed to Phoolan Devi to teach these Thakurs a lesson. She had her own reasons as well. Her lover Bikram Singh had been murdered by Thakurs Lal Ram Singh and his twin brother Shri Ram Singh. And they had kept her imprisoned in this village for several weeks raping and beating her. She managed to escape and rejoin her gang. She also suspected that these fellows have been informing the police of her movements. It was revenge, pure and simple.'

'For every man this girl has killed, she has slept with two,' said the superintendent of police in charge of 'Operation Phoolan Devi'. The police estimate the number of men slain by her or one of her gang in the last year and a half to be over thirty. There is no way of finding out the exact number of men she murdered or was laid by. But it is certain that not all the killings nor the copulations were entirely of her own choosing. On many occasions she happened to be with bandits who were trigger-happy; and being the only woman in a gang of a dozen or more, she was regarded by them as their common property. She accepted the rules of the game and had to give herself to them in turn. It was more a resignation to being raped than the craving for sex of a nymphomaniac.

I was able to reconstruct Phoolan Devi's past by talking to her parents, sisters and one of her lovers, and cross-checking what they told me with a statement she made to the police on 6 January 1979, the first time she was arrested. This was in connection with a robbery in the house of her cousin with whom her father had had a dispute over land. Some stolen goods were recovered from her. She spent a fortnight in police custody. Her statement is prefaced by a noting made by the officer. He describes her as 'about twenty years old; wheatish complexion, oval face; short but sturdily built.' Phoolan Devi stated: 'I am the second daughter of a family of six consisting of five girls. The youngest is a boy, Shiv Narain Singh. We belong to the Mallah caste and live in the village Gurh-ka-Purwa. At the age of twelve I was given away in marriage to a forty-five-year-old widower, Putti Lal.' Then she talks of her second 'marriage' to Kailash in Kanpur. The rest of her life story was narrated to me by her mother, Muli. 'Phoolan Devi was too young to consummate her marriage and came back to us after a few days. A year or two later, we sent her back to her husband. This time she stayed with him for a few months but was unhappy. She came away without her husband's permission, determined not to go back to him.' It would appear that she had been deflowered. Her mother describes her as being 'filled up'—an Indian expression for a girl whose bosom and behind indicate that she has had sex. It would appear that she had developed an appetite for sex which her ageing husband could not fulfil. Her parents were distraught: a girl leaving her husband brought disgrace to the family. 'I told her to drop dead,' said her mother. 'I told her to jump in a well or drown herself in the Jamuna; we would not have a married daughter living with us. Putti Lal came and took away the silver ornaments he had given her and married another woman. What were we to do? We started looking for another husband for her, but it is not easy to find a husband for a discarded girl, is it?' she asked me. Phoolan Devi kept out of her parents' way as much as she could by taking the family's buffaloes out for grazing. She began to liaise with the son of the village headman. (In rural India such affairs are consummated in lentil or sugarcane fields.) The headman's son invited his friends to partake of the feast. Phoolan Devi had no choice but to give in. The village gossip mill ground out stories of Phoolan Devi being available to anyone who wanted to lay her. Her mother admitted, 'The family's pojeeshun (position) was compromised; our noses were cut. We decided to send her away to her sister, Ramkali, who lives in Teonga village across the river.'

It did not take long for Phoolan Devi to find another lover in Teonga. This was a distant cousin, Kailash, married and with four children. Kailash had contacts with a dacoit gang. He gives a vivid account of how he was seduced by Phoolan Devi. 'One day I was washing my clothes on the banks of the Jamuna. This girl brought her sister's buffaloes to wallow in the shallows of the river. We got talking. She asked me to lend her my cake of soap so that she could bathe herself. I gave her what remained of the soap. She stripped herself before my eyes. While she splashed water on herself and soaped her bosom and buttocks, she kept talking to me. I got very excited watching her. After she was dressed, I followed her into the lentil fields. I threw her on the ground and mounted her. I was too worked up and was finished in no time. I begged her to meet me again.' She agreed to come the next day at the same time and at the same place.

'We made love many times. But it was never enough. She started playing hard to get.'

'If you want me, you must marry me. Then I'll give you all you want,' she said. I told her I had a wife and children and could only have her as my mistress. She would not let me touch her unless I agreed to marry her. I became desperate. I took her with me to Kanpur. A lawyer took fifty rupees from me, wrote something on a piece of paper and told us that we were man and wife. We spent two days in Kanpur. During the day we went to the movies; at night we made love and slept in each other's arms. When we returned to Teonga, my parents refused to take us in. We spent a night out in the fields. The next day I told Phoolan Devi to go back to her parents as I had decided to return to my wife and children. She swore she would kill me. I have not seen her since. But I am afraid one of these days she will get me.'

'What does your Phoolania look like?' I asked Kailash. 'I am told her sister Ramkali resembles her.'

'Phoolan is slightly shorter, lighter-skinned and has a nicer figure. She is much better-looking than Ramkali.'

'I am told she uses very bad language.'

'She never spoke harshly to me; to me she spoke only the language of love.'

Phoolan Devi had more coming to her. A few days after she had been turned out by Kailash, she ran into Kailash's wife Shanti, at a village fair. Shanti pounced on Phoolan, tore her hair, clawed her face and in front of the crowd that had collected, abused her: 'Whore! Bitch! Homebreaker!' What was known only to a few hamlets now became common knowledge: Phoolan was a slut. As if this were not enough, the village headman's son, who was under the impression that Phoolan was exclusively at his beck and call, heard of her escapade with Kailash. He summoned her to his house and thrashed her with his shoes. Thus, at the age of eighteen, Phoolan found herself discarded by everyone. Her parents did not want her, her old husband had divorced her, her second 'marriage' had come to naught, she had been laid by men, none of whom was willing to take her as a wife. It seemed to her that no one in the world wanted to have anything to do with her. She had only two choices before her: to go to some distant city and become a prostitute, or kill herself. There were times she considered throwing herself into the well.

Unknown to her, there was someone who had taken a fancy to her. This was young Bikram Singh, a friend of Kailash and member of a gang of dacoits led by a man called Babu Gujjar. Bikram Singh had seen Phoolan around the village and heard stories of her performances in the lentil fields. One afternoon he came to Gurh-ka-Purwa with some of his gang and bluntly told Phoolan's parents that he had come to take away their daughter. Phoolan was adamant. 'I will talk to you with my sandals,' she said spitting on the ground. Bikram hit her with a whip he was carrying. Phoolan Devi fled from the village and went to stay with her other sister, Rukmini, in the village Orai. It was there that she heard that a warrant for arrest had been issued against her and Kailash for the dacoity in her cousin's house. The man who took her to the police station raped her before handing her over. She spent a fortnight in jail. When she returned home, Bikram came to see her again. He threatened her: 'Either you come with me or I take your brother Shiv Narain with me.' Phoolan was very attached to her only brother; he was eleven years old and studying in the village school. After some wrangling, she agreed to go with Bikram.

Kailash describes Bikram Singh as fair, tall and wiry. Bikram was obviously very taken with Phoolan. He had her long hair cropped. He gave her a transistor radio and cassette recorder as she was inordinately fond of listening to film music. He bought her a khaki shirt and jeans. He taught her how to handle a gun. She proved a very adept disciple and was soon a crack shot.

For the first time in her life Phoolan felt wanted by someone. She responded to Bikram's affection and began to describe herself as his beloved. She had a rubber stamp made for herself which she used as a letterhead in the letters she got written on her behalf. It reads: 'Dasyu Sundari, Dasyu Samrat Bikram Singh ki Premika' (Dacoit Beauty, Beloved of Bikram Singh, the King of Dacoits).

Being the 'beloved of Bikram' did not confer any special privileges on Phoolan. Whether she liked it or not, she had to serve the rest of the gang. At the time, the leader happened to be Babu Gujjar, a singularly rough customer. He had his own way of expressing his superiority over his gang. He liked to have sex in broad daylight and in front of the others. So Phoolan Devi had to submit to being ravished and brutalized by Babu Gujjar in public. When her turn came to be made love to by Bikram, she complained to him about the indignity. By then, Bikram had developed a strong sense of possession over Phoolan. He did not have the courage to admit it, but one night while Babu Gujjar was asleep, he shot him in the head. Bikram Singh became the leader of the gang and at Phoolan's insistence, forbade the others from touching her. There wasn't much resentment because the gang soon acquired another woman, Kusum Nain, who happened to be better-looking than Phoolan. Kusum, a Thakur, attached herself to the Thakur brothers, Lal Ram Singh and Shri Ram Singh. The two women became jealous of each other.

Despite her many unpleasant experiences with men, Phoolan Devi did not give up her habit of cock-teasing. She sensed that her full bosom and rounded buttocks set men's minds aflame with lust. Nevertheless, she persisted in bathing in the presence of the men of her gang. One gangster, now in police custody, who had known her as well as Kusum Nain and Meera Thakur (other female dacoits, since then slain) vouches for this: 'The other girls were as tough as Phoolan but they observed certain proprieties in the company of men. They would go behind a tree or bushes to take a bath. Not Phoolan; she took off her clothes in front of us as if we did not exist. The other girls used language becoming to women. Phoolan is the most foul-mouthed wench I have ever met. Every time she opens her mouth she uses the foulest of abuse—bhosreekey, gaandu (bugger), madarchod, betichod (daughterfucker).'

The inspector of police has in his files a sheaf of letters written to him on behalf of Phoolan Devi. They are a delightful mixture of the sacred and the profane, of highfalutin Hindi and sheer obscenity. The one he read out to me began with salutations to the Mother Goddess under her printed letterhead. The text ran somewhat as follows:

Honourable and Respected Inspector General Sahib,

I learn from several Hindi journals that you have been making speeches saying that you will have us dacoits shot like pie-dogs. I hereby give you notice that if you do not stop bakwas (nonsense) of this kind, I will have your revered mother abducted and so thoroughly fucked by my men that she will need medical attention. So take heed.

It is more than likely that Bikram Singh, besides keeping Phoolan Devi exclusively for himself, also claimed his right as the leader, to enjoy the company of Kusum Nain as well. This irked the Thakur brothers. They left Bikram's gang and looked out for an opportunity to kill him. On the night of 13 August 1980, they trapped and slew Bikram Singh. It is believed that the murder was committed in Behmai, and that the Thakurs unceremoniously kicked Bikram's corpse before it was thrown into the river.

Lal Ram Singh and Shri Ram Singh retained Phoolan Devi in Behmai. They brutalized and humiliated her in front of the entire village. One night, on the pretext of wanting to relieve herself, Phoolan Devi managed to vanish into the darkness. She crossed the Jamuna over to the Mallah village, Pal. From there she got in touch with the Muslim gangster Baba Mustaqeem and pleaded with him to help her avenge the murder of Bikram Singh. Mustaqeem agreed. This is how she ended up being at Behmai on the afternoon of 14 February 1981.

GHAYOORUNNISA HAFEEZ

Ghayoorunnisa Hafeez of Hyderabad came into my life when I was seventeen years old. She was a couple of years older and had come to Delhi to join Lady Hardinge Medical College where her elder sister was studying.

After a year of medical studies she joined Lady Irwin College to take a degree in home science. My younger sister was a student there. The two girls became friends. She was invited to our home for a weekend.

She came draped in a burkha. At my sister's insistence she took it off and was introduced to the family. For me it was a bewitching experience. The art of unveiling is a dramatic event, as spectacular as when a curtain goes up in a theatre revealing a stage brightly lit with coloured lights, resembling a fairyland.

My first impression was that she was beautiful beyond compare. She was a small, frail girl with a sallow complexion and curly light brown hair. She spoke English without any regional accent. Her Urdu was delightfully Dabhhani, What really bowled me over was that a girl who had spent so many of her adolescent years in seclusion could be so saucy and forward.

A few days after she came to our home for the first time, my sister and I took her to the pictures. I sat between the two girls. No sooner were the lights dimmed than she took my hand under the folds of her sari. I was wild with joy.

She once got permission to spend an evening at our home. I went to pick her up and instead of taking her home, I took her for a long drive around New Delhi. At that time it was still sparsely populated and the ridge was a welcome wilderness. We never got beyond holding hands and exchanging words of affection. She was very firm about how far unmarried people could go in getting to know each other.

We wrote long letters to each other. We continued writing to each other in the years I was in England. Her letters got shorter and rarer and then stopped altogether. I learnt from my sister that Ghayoor had got married to a Muslim army officer who also belonged to Hyderabad.

Why I regard my brief and near-platonic relationship with Ghayoor an important landmark in my life is because it changed my attitude towards Muslims.

Like other Hindus and Sikhs of my generation, I had been brought up on anti-Muslim prejudices based on Muslim stereotypes.

The first awakening came with my close association with the saintly maulvi Shaifuddin Nayyar, my Urdu teacher. A more upright and God-fearing man I had not met in my childhood.

Then came Ghayoorunnisa Hafeez who proved to me that members of the two communities could love each other. Once you fall in love with someone of another community, you fall in love with all her people. And finally there was Manzur Qadir. After coming to know these people, I came to the naïve conclusion that an Indian Muslim could do no wrong.

Ghayoorunnisa resurfaced in my life thirty years later. My sister had asked me over for breakfast at my parents' home. When I arrived there she asked me, 'Do you recognize this girl?' Of course! It was Ghayoor. She was no longer a girl but a middle-aged woman who had buried two husbands. With her was a comely teenager,

Fareesa, her daughter from her first husband. Fareesa joined Lady Irwin College. I was appointed her local guardian. Fareesa was very popular with college boys. Whenever she went out with them she left a note saying that she was going to see her local guardian. She had no problem extracting a letter from me stating that she had spent the evening in my home.

Fareesa spent her first honeymoon with her English husband at my house. She later divorced him and married a Swedish banker. They live in style in Hong Kong. Whenever I am in Hong Kong I stay with her. To her children from her two husbands, I am 'nana'—maternal grandfather.

Once having re-established contact with Ghayoor, I never lost it. Every time I go to Hyderabad, we spend our evenings together. She has become very frail and nearly blind. She has also become very religious.

It is five prayers a day and a daily appeal to Allah to send for her. The last time I was in Hyderabad, I had to track her down to an old ladies' home.

She took me to a dargah where her parents and sisters are buried. She has reserved a site for her own grave. 'I paid Rs 1,500 for it fifteen years ago. Today this would cost more than Rs 15,000,' she told me. 'Why don't you sell it and make a profit?' I said trying to cheer her up. She turned down the suggestion.

'I have had salt sprinkled on the grave. It is a Hyderabadi custom, and no one else besides me can be buried there.'

As I was leaving, Ghayoor said, 'I have no one left in the world who bothers about me except you. Fareesa is involved with her own family and hardly ever writes to me. My parents and all my sisters are dead. Why does Allah not listen to my prayers and send for me? I don't want to live any longer.'

SADIA DEHLVI

It was in 1987 at Amina Ahuja's calligraphy exhibition, that I first met her. 'Come, let me introduce you to Sadia Dehlvi,' said Amina taking me by my hand and leading me to a girl sitting on a morha in the middle of a crowded room. The girl didn't bother to get up. She simply gaped at me with her large, luscious eyes. Her jet-black hair cascaded in curls around her oval face. There was nothing I could think of saying to her except blurting out, 'Why are you so beautiful?'

Her face flushed with joy as she put out her hand and replied, 'If you think I am beautiful, I must be beautiful', or words to that effect. I had not caught her name and asked her to tell me again. 'Sadia Dehlvi,' she replied. 'You must have heard of the Dehlvis of the

Sharma group of journals. I am Yunus Dehlvi's daughter. I edit an Urdu magazine, *Bano*.'

I spent an hour talking to her. I invited her to my home to meet my family. From that day to the time she married Reza Parvez and left for Pakistan, Sadia remained my closest friend. Our age difference did not matter at all. Nor the fact that she came from a conservative Muslim family well-known in northern India and that I, an aged Sikh, was often described by the gutter press as the 'dirty old man of Delhi'. Although often seen with me, I meant to keep our friendship to ourselves. Not Sadia. She proclaimed from the house tops and in interviews to Bombay's gossip magazines that 'the only man in my life is Khushwant Singh.'

Sadia was emotionally very promiscuous. And utterly outspoken. She talked to me by the hour telling me of the many men in her life. She had made a disastrous marriage with the scion of a family that ran the leading Urdu daily in Calcutta. Her husband had been mother-fixated and prone to violence. She divorced him and returned to her parents' home. She was a restless character, ever changing her jobs and admirers. She would open a boutique one day, talk of the millions she would make in a few months and then close it after a few days to start a furniture business. She would take a franchise in a restaurant and give it up in a few days to make bigger millions by exporting carpets.

For a while she toyed with the idea of getting into politics. She led a march to Meerut where communal riots had broken out, and tried to nurse Jamia Nagar and Zakir Bagh which had sizeable Muslim populations, as her constituency. She went abroad a few times. Once in England she ran out of money and worked as a barmaid in a pub serving beer to customers. To atone for her 'sins', on her way back to India, she broke journey to perform an Umra pilgrimage at Mecca and Medina. She had a natural flair for writing, and was commissioned by *India Today* as well as *The Times of India* to write regular columns for them. No one could have asked for a bigger break. Her enthusiasm lasted a few weeks. She quickly got bored with anything she did. One time she took to riding and then decided to learn flying instead. She hired a maulvi sahib to teach her Persian and Arabic. Then the zest for living got the better of the desire to become a scholar. She loved animals and once bought a cuddly little cocker spaniel. Then one day she dumped it in the flat of her then closest girl friend, Kamna Prasad, promising to pick it up later that evening. Three days later Kamna had to deposit the pup in Sadia's home.

Sadia had a grasshopper's personality. Above everyone else, she loved herself. Once she was in the press party that accompanied Rajiv Gandhi on a foreign tour. Being much the most photogenic in the group next to the prime minister, she attracted more attention on television and in the media. For a while she toyed with the idea of joining the Congress party and getting into one or the other houses of Parliament, but soon got bored with the idea.

One thing Sadia was consistent about was wanting to get married. More than marriage, she wanted to be a mother. Her husband had to be Muslim. The father of her child had to be Muslim. When the late Ismat Chughtai advised her to be bold and produce a bastard ('Haraamee paida kar'), Sadia was appalled.

Many eligible men proposed marriage to her. She gave them bhaav but never her hand in marriage. Ultimately it was Reza Parvez, almost twenty years older than her, divorced father of two grown-up children and a Shia (Sadia is Sunni), who wore down Sadia's resistance. Her mother kept telling her right till the day of her wedding, that if she wanted to change her mind, she could do so before signing the nikahnamah. She did not change her mind. I signed the nikahnamah as a witness to her consent to marry Reza. I thought Sadia would take Pakistani citizenship and go out of my life. Once again I had misjudged her.

A few months after Sadia and Reza had settled down in Islamabad to what appeared to me blissful and happy matrimony, they came to meet me in Lahore where I had been invited to deliver the Manzur Qadir Memorial Lecture on Indo–Pak relations. Sadia came to the lecture dressed in a gorgeous sari. Pakistani women invariably wore salwar-kameez. Sadia sported a red bindi on her forehead. In Pakistan this was the sign of kufr (heresy) worn by infidels. She had become aggressively Indian in a country which regarded India as enemy number one. In course of time, a Pakistani rag denounced Sadia as an Indian spy. She became persona non grata in Pakistani society. Reza was fired from his job.

Sadia was confused and unhappy. Far from being a Grihalakshmi, she had brought misfortune on her husband's household. She was back in Delhi looking for a job and seeing gynaecologists wanting to know why she had not conceived. Reza, she confided to me, was a great lover. The couple returned to Pakistan. Reza had to sell his house in Karachi to keep the home fires burning. Slowly the wheel of fortune turned in their favour. Reza found a job; Sadia was pregnant. A son was born to them. They named him Armaan. Six months later Sadia brought Armaan to meet his real grandfather—me. She chided me for not having dedicated any book to her. So I did. *Not a Nice Man to Know* bears the dedication: 'To Sadia Dehlvi who gave me more affection and notoriety than I deserved.'

ANEES JUNG

꧁

If I had to draw a list of the most engaging conversationalists I have met in my life, Anees Jung's name would feature right at the top. Even though I am never sure that what she tells me is true or a figment of her fantasies.

She could flatter any man out of his wits, then run him down while talking to others. And if confronted, flatly deny having done so. She does it to me all the time and yet I look forward to being with her. She is a good hostess, serves gourmet food and vintage wines. She often has well-known singers to entertain her guests. She is an incorrigible name-dropper, but the amazing truth is that she does in fact know all the names she drops.

To her home come presidents of the Republic, Cabinet ministers, leaders of the Opposition, governors, national figures, poets, writers, ambassadors and counsellors.

The paradigm for human beings according to her, is what she describes as the 'Renaissance gentleman': well-dressed, sophisticated, au courant with the arts, literature and lifestyle. Her self-image is that of a Renaissance lady who gathers men around her. Where did I fit in her scheme of things?

Well, I was the first to give her a job. I have known her for over thirty years. And though often exasperated by her go-getting ways and saying nasty things about people behind their backs, I could never drop her. She took good care that I did not do so.

Sometime in the early 1960s, she returned with a degree from some American university. She rang up my wife to say that she had met our son in Bombay and he had suggested that she get in touch with his parents when she was in Delhi. She was promptly invited to lunch. Both of us were charmed by her. She bore an aristocratic, Hyderabadi name, 'Jung'.

She spoke English without a trace of an American accent and Hindustani in the Dakkhani lilt and the genders all mixed up which I find very attractive. She was looking for a job. I had a temporary one to offer. I was conducting a party of American students around the world. Two months were to be spent in India. We had completed one month in Delhi. The second was to be in Hyderabad. The boys and girls had to be put up with Hyderabadi families and lectures arranged for them. Anees was a Hyderabadi who knew the best families in the city. She accepted the job at what was then a handsome remuneration. She executed her assignment with dispatch and found excellent homes for all my students getting top academics like Professor Rashiduddin, MP, to speak to them. At the same time, instead of one Delhi–Hyderabad–Delhi air trip, she made me pay for three. She got under the skin of the family she was staying with and was unceremoniously thrown out. Far from being crushed, she bounced back to life and made her presence felt in the city.

Whenever she came to see me in any hotel, she drove up in the American Consul-General's big limousine. At a dinner reception hosted by this diplomat, she overshadowed all the others present. Many guests got the impression she was closely connected with the family of the Nizam of Hyderabad.

Actually, Anees Jung's ancestors were not from Hyderabad but from Lucknow. Her father, Hoshiar, migrated to Hyderabad and soon attracted the Nizam's attention. He was a very cultivated man with a gift for words. Though never formally given an official position, he was given the title 'Nawab', and became a very close companion masahib of His Exalted Highness and was granted a large haveli and other real estate in the city.

The family lived in feudal splendour till, for reasons unknown, he fell out of favour and lost most of what he had. Nothing now remains of Nawab Hoshiar Jung's wealth. However, Anees can be forgiven for believing that her father was a minister—even prime minister—of Hyderabad.

Being go-getting is Anees's second nature. Once when I was invited to Guwahati, a Canadian woman, Sue Dexter (over six feet tall), who wanted to see as much of India as she could in a fortnight, asked me if she could come along with me. I agreed that she could but warned her that I had many engagements in Guwahati and would not have much time to take her around. Also that she would have to find her own accommodation as I would be staying in the Circuit House. She asked Anees, whose sister she knew, to come along as her escort, all expenses paid. We arrived at Guwahati to a guard of honour presented by the Khalsa High School and a band playing the national anthem. The two women came to the Circuit House with me. Sue Dexter found a room in a small hotel. Anees rang up the Governor, B.K. Nehru, and told him she was a friend of his son and did not know where to stay in Guwahati. She was invited to stay at the Raj Bhavan.

For the next three days, the three of us rode in the Governor's car to see the sights along the Brahmaputra.

Her muscling in on President Zail Singh's visit to Bombay to inspect the Indian Navy was even more audacious. When I told her I had been invited by Gianiji to accompany him, she simply rang up Rashtrapati Bhavan and told the president's secretary, that she would be coming along as well.

We flew in the president's private plane. While I stayed in a hotel, Anees was a guest of Governor Ali Yavar Jung. She flew back on the same plane. President Zail Singh was enchanted by her bada gharana upbringing and impeccable manners. Every Eid, a presidential hamper of fruit was delivered at her flat.

I had many opportunities of seeing Anees Jung when I was editing *The Illustrated Weekly of India*. The board of Bennett Coleman wanted to launch a magazine for the young. I was involved in the decision taken regarding the choice of editor. I chose Anees Jung. *Youth Times* was based in Delhi. But within a few weeks Anees had become a great favourite of the board, particularly with the general manager, Mr Ram Tarneja.

She was in and out of Bombay whenever she wished. Every evening she would be seen sitting in the back of Tarneja's car parked in the portico. All the staff going home viewed her as the most privileged of editors of *The Times of India* group of papers.

I was very put off and decided to have nothing to do with her. For a couple of years after being thrown out of *The Illustrated Weekly of India*, I refused to speak to her. At a reception in the house of the Pakistani High Commissioner, she came to sit near me. I got up and took another seat. 'So it is still like that,' she remarked and went into a sulk.

Youth Times didn't survive. Anees was once again out of a job. Then for the first time she thought of doing some serious writing. Everyone was surprised to find she had a talent for good, straight and very evocative writing. I don't recall how we got together again, but she was with me when I went to Amritsar in June 1984 to see the havoc wrought by the Indian Army in Operation Bluestar. It was not I, a Sikh, but Anees Jung, a Shia Muslim, who kept making offerings of flowers, money and prasaad at every shrine we visited.

It would be unfair to describe Anees Jung as matlabee, a seeker of favours. Her columns in *The Times of India* gave her an all-India readership. She has published many books, and *Unveiling India* went into many editions, opening up several avenues for her. She got a lucrative assignment from the UN to do a definitive book on the status of women in Asia. It was released at the UN conference on population in Cairo. She is currently with the UNESCO and is a voice for Asian women.

I haven't met another woman quite like Anees Jung, and I am tempted to write a novel with her as the central character.

THE PORTRAIT OF A LADY

My grandmother, like everybody's grandmother, was an old woman. She had been old and wrinkled for the twenty years that I had known her. People said that she had once been young and pretty, and had even had a husband, but that was hard to believe. My grandfather's portrait hung above the mantelpiece in the drawing-room. He wore a big turban and loose-fitting clothes. His long white beard covered the best part of his chest and he looked at least a hundred years old. He did not look the sort of person who would have a wife or children. He looked as if he could only have lots and lots of grandchildren. As for my grandmother being young and pretty, the thought was almost revolting. She often told us of the games she used to play as a child. That seemed quite absurd and undignified on her part and we treated it like the fables of the Prophets she used to tell us.

She had always been short and fat and slightly bent. Her face was a criss-cross of wrinkles running from everywhere to everywhere. No, we were certain she had always been as we had known her. Old, so terribly old that she could not have grown older, and had stayed at the same age for twenty years. She could never have been pretty; but she was always beautiful. She hobbled about the house in spotless white with one hand resting on her waist to balance her stoop and the other telling the beads of her rosary. Her silver locks were scattered untidily over her pale, puckered face, and her lips constantly moved in inaudible prayer. Yes, she was beautiful. She was like the winter landscape in the mountains, an expanse of pure white serenity breathing peace and contentment.

My grandmother and I were good friends. My parents left me with her when they went to live in the city and we were constantly together. She used to wake me up in the morning and get me ready for school. She said her morning prayer in a monotonous sing-song while she bathed and dressed me in the hope that I would listen and get to know it by heart. I listened because I loved her voice but never bothered to learn it. Then she would fetch my wooden slate which she had already washed and plastered with yellow chalk, a tiny earthen inkpot and a reed pen, tie them all in a bundle and hand it to me. After a breakfast of a thick, stale chapatti with a little butter and sugar spread on it, we went to school. She carried several stale chapatties with her for the village dogs.

My grandmother always went to school with me because the school was attached to the temple. The priest taught us the alphabet and the morning prayer. While the children sat in rows on either side of the veranda singing the alphabet or the prayer in a chorus, my grandmother sat inside reading the scriptures. When we had both finished, we would walk back together. This time the village dogs would meet us at the temple door. They followed us to our home growling and fighting each other for the chapatties we threw to them.

When my parents were comfortably settled in the city, they sent for us. That was a turning point in our friendship. Although we shared the same room, my grandmother no longer came to school with me. I used to go to an English school in a motor bus. There were no dogs in the streets and she took to feeding sparrows in the courtyard of our city house.

As the years rolled by we saw less of each other. For some time she continued to wake me up and get me ready for school. When I came back she would ask me what the teacher had taught me. I would tell her English words and little things of Western science and learning, the law of gravity, Archimedes's principle, the world being round, etc. This made her unhappy. She could not help me with my lessons. She did not believe in the things they taught at the English school and was distressed that there was no teaching about God and the scriptures. One day I announced that we were being given music lessons. She was very disturbed. To her music had lewd associations. It was the monopoly of harlots and beggars and not meant for gentle folk. She rarely talked to me after that.

When I went up to University, I was given a room of my own.

The common link of friendship was snapped. My grandmother accepted her seclusion with resignation. She rarely left her spinning wheel to talk to anyone. From sunrise to sunset she sat by her wheel, spinning and reciting prayers. Only in the afternoon she relaxed for a while to feed the sparrows. While she sat in the veranda breaking the bread into little bits, hundreds of little birds collected round her, creating a veritable bedlam of chirrupings. Some came and perched on her legs, others on her shoulders. Some even sat on her head. She smiled but never shooed them away. It used to be the happiest half-hour of the day for her.

When I decided to go abroad for further studies, I was sure my grandmother would be upset. I would be away for five years, and at her age one could never tell. But my grandmother could. She was not even sentimental. She came to leave me at the railway station but did not talk or show any emotion. Her lips moved in prayer, her mind was lost in prayer. Her fingers were busy telling the beads of her rosary. Silently she kissed my forehead, and when I left I cherished the moist imprint as perhaps the last sign of physical contact between us.

But that was not so. After five years I came back home and was met by her at the station. She did not look a day older. She still had no time for words, and while she clasped me in her arms I could hear her reciting her prayer. Even on the first day of my arrival, her happiest moments were with her sparrows whom she fed longer and with frivolous rebukes.

In the evening a change came over her. She did not pray. She collected the women of the neighbourhood, got an old drum and started to sing. For several hours she thumped the sagging skins of the dilapidated drum and sang of the home-coming of warriors. We had to persuade her to stop to avoid overstraining. That was the first time since I had known her that she did not pray.

The next morning she was taken ill. It was a mild fever and the doctor told us that it would go. But my grandmother thought differently. She told us that her end was near. She said that, since only a few hours before the close of the last chapter of her life she had omitted to pray, she was not going to waste any more time talking to us.

We protested. But she ignored our protests. She lay peacefully in bed praying and telling her beads. Even before we could suspect, her lips stopped moving and the rosary fell from her lifeless fingers. A peaceful pallor spread on her face and we knew that she was dead.

AMRITA SHER-GIL

❧

Women seduce. That is a fact. I have been seduced by women all my life, right from the time I was attracted to my first love, Ghayoor—it was she who had held my hand. Most women have made the first pass at me, led me on, with the exception of two women, wherein I took the lead. Even when I was attracted to a woman, I had little confidence to make the first move; instead, I was terribly flattered when women made a pass at me. Looking back, I wish I had the confidence to make the first move, for I could have got closer to several women, like the now legendary painter Amrita Sher-Gil. Amrita, you see, had threatened to seduce me. It happened in Shimla in the mid-1930s. Amrita came into my sitting room (and my life) one day and introduced herself. She told me of the flat she had rented across the road, and wanted advice about carpenters, plumbers, tailors and the like. I tried to size her up. I couldn't look her in the face too long because she had that bold, brazen kind of look that makes timid men like me turn their gaze down. She was short and sallow-complexioned (being half Sikh and half Hungarian). Her hair was parted in the middle and tightly bound at the back. She had a bulbous nose, with blackheads showing. She had thick lips with a faint shadow of a moustache. Politeness, I discovered, was not one of her virtues; she believed in speaking her mind, however rude or unkind it be.

As a baby, my son, Rahul, was in the playpen, learning to stand on his feet. Everyone was paying him compliments: he was a very pretty little child with curly hair, large, questioning eyes and dimpled cheeks. 'What an ugly little boy!' remarked Amrita. Others protested their embarrassment. My wife froze. Amrita continued to drink her beer without concern.

There were stories that Amrita had seduced many well-known characters of that time. People like the art critic Karl Khandalawala, Iqbal Singh and her nephew, the painter Vivan Sundaram, have written books on Amrita; Badruddin Tyebji has given a vivid account of how he was seduced by her—she simply took off her clothes and lay herself naked on the carpet by the fireplace. Vivan Sundaram, Amrita's nephew, admits to her having many lovers; according to him, her real passion in life was another woman.

Unfortunately, Amrita couldn't carry out her threat of seducing me because she died a few months later. She was not yet thirty then.

BEGUM PARA

In the early 1970s, I visited Pakistan twice to see how Zulfiqar Ali Bhutto was doing, and how Pakistan was taking the drubbing of its army by the Indian forces in the 1971 war. The second of these visits turned out more interesting, as among the people I met was Begum Para. That meeting has remained one of my most memorable encounters.

I had first met Begum Para through Rukhsana Sultana, who was her niece and married to my nephew. One-time super-vamp of the Indian screen, Begum Para had put on a lot of weight after she married Nasir Khan (brother of superstar Yusuf Khan, a.k.a, Dilip Kumar). She had borne him two lovely children—a daughter and a son—and I had met them several times in Bombay when she was living there. Many a Sunday morning, the family would join me at the Gymkhana Club bathing pool to swim and have breakfast.

When Nasir died, he left behind very little besides a flat in Bandra and a couple of films. Now, Begum Para felt that she had a right to some of the millions that her brother-in-law was making; however, this was to no avail. So she frequently brought up the question of money: if anyone could loan her forty or fifty thousand rupees, she would say, she could have her old films rescreened and make a fortune. I didn't take the hint.

In sheer desperation, Begum Para eventually abandoned Bombay for Pakistan, where she had a considerable inheritance waiting to be claimed. But it didn't take her long to discover that her relatives were not willing to part with anything, and she was on weak ground, having earlier opted for India. She earned a little by flogging films she had brought with her and appearing on television. Her children too were unhappy; after the free and easy atmosphere of Bombay, the girl, who was rapidly growing into a beautiful young lady, found the puritanical atmosphere of Pakistan particularly stifling. They wanted rather badly to return to Bombay.

Begum Para had written me several letters, asking

for help in returning to India; I wrote back that I would be visiting Karachi soon and we could talk the matter over.

When I arrived in Karachi early in the evening, Begum Para and her children were at the airport to receive me. So was the chief of protocol, as I was a guest of the government. We were conducted to the VIP lounge, where the children had their fill of cakes and biscuits. Once they were sent home, Begum Para accepted my invitation to dine with me at the hotel where I was to stay the night. The chief of protocol dropped us at my hotel, and Begum Para accompanied me to my room.

I ordered soda and ice and took out the bottle of Scotch I had brought with me. There was, at that time, no prohibition in Pakistan. I had heard stories about Begum Para's drinking problem; she had apparently been forced to cut down on it because of the price: a bottle of Scotch cost twice as much in Pakistan as it did in India.

'Would you like a drink?' I asked her, unsure whether she was still a drinking woman.

'I'll take a little,' she replied. 'I haven't seen genuine Scotch for ages.'

I poured out two stiff whiskies and handed her one.

I was not even halfway through my glass when I saw that hers was empty. I poured her another one, which she tossed back instantly; I had to refill her glass once more before I resumed my own drinking.

By the time I had finished my quota of three large whiskies, Begum Para had had nine and the bottle was almost empty. I told her then that we must eat soon as I had to catch the early-morning flight to Islamabad. Reluctantly, she got up to go with me to the dining room.

The dining room was on the first floor and we had to climb up a spiral marble staircase to get to it. The place was crowded, but, as was usual in Pakistan, there were very few women there. People recognized Begum Para because of her appearances on television. It was quite evident that they were intrigued to see her in the company of a Sikh. She had another two whiskies before the soup was served. She had begun to slur over her words and her eyes had taken on a glazed look. She wanted to have yet another drink with her meal, but I put my foot down.

At long last, the meal came to an end and I got up to assist Begum Para with her chair. She stood up, swayed a little and collapsed on the carpet. The waiters came running to help her get back to her feet. I took her arm to help her walk to the stairs. All eyes in the dining room had turned to us, and I was doubly careful going down the spiral staircase. I gripped her fat arm. 'One step at a time,' I instructed her. We finally made it to the foyer. I ordered a taxi for her and waited patiently for the ordeal to be over.

A taxi drew up in the portico. I gave the driver a hundred-rupee note and told him to take the lady home. He recognized Begum Para and knew where she lived. I opened the rear door of the taxi and went back to help her. As she stepped forward, she missed her step and, once again, collapsed on the ground, this time with a loud fart. She had sprained her ankle and began to howl in pain: 'Hai rabba, main mar gayee!'—Oh God, I'm dead!

A crowd had gathered, but no one came forward to help. Being an Islamic country, no unrelated male could touch a woman. I did my best to haul Begum Para up to her feet by myself. She was far too heavy for me. I pleaded with the taxi driver for help. My advance tip came in handy—he acquiesced. Together, we got Begum Para on her feet and pushed her into the seat. I slammed the door shut and bid her a hurried farewell, swearing to forever steer clear of divas given to drink. That was my last encounter with Begum Para. But when I heard of her passing in 2008, I was deeply saddened, remembering only the pleasure of those shared Sunday breakfasts long ago in Bombay.

INDIRA GANDHI

In 2009, the twenty-fifth death anniversary of Indira Gandhi occasioned a flood of literature and huge media coverage across the country. That was as it should have been because she was, in fact, the Queen Empress of India for long years and changed the face of the country by ruthless plastic surgery. She made the Congress subservient to her wishes, nationalized banks, deprived princely families of their unearned privy purses, inflicted a humiliating defeat on Pakistan and liberated Bangladesh. Dev Kant Baruah was not much off the mark when he hailed her thus: 'India is Indira, Indira is India. Tere naam ki jai! Tere kaam ki jai!' However, it must not be forgotten that there were two distinct sides to her character—the public persona, and the private. She was a great public leader, but at the same time she was very petty in her private life. She was undoubtedly a most beautiful woman, but she disliked other good-looking women and humiliated them, among whom were Tarakeshwari Sinha and Maharani Gayatri Devi. And the number of people she and her family put behind bars during the Emergency makes one sick. But she was able to get away with what she did because India's poor millions loved her as 'Amma'—Mother.

I first met her when she was still unmarried and had stopped in Lahore on her way to Kashmir. I must have been about eighteen years old then. Indira was staying with friends who brought her over to our house. She appeared very shy and would not talk much. I remember thinking of her as a 'goongi gudiya'—a mute doll. Years later, when I met her in Delhi, she did not seem to recollect that meeting, though I have pictures of her at our house.

Indira Gandhi was a very good-looking woman—not the pin-up kind but an indescribable aristocratic type. She reminded me of Hilaire Belloc's lines:

Her face was like the King's command
When all the swords are drawn

I have been asked if I ever wanted to get close to her in the physical sense; the answer is no. There was something cold and haughty about her. Not my type at all, for I like women who are vivacious and spontaneous. But she had her set of admirers. Amongst the many men who were bowled over by her looks was President Lyndon Johnson of the United States. Just before a dinner hosted by the Indian ambassador B.K. Nehru and his wife for Indira, at which Vice President Hubert Humphrey was to be the guest of honour, Lyndon Johnson stayed on tossing glass after glass of bourbon on the rocks while talking to Indira. He readily agreed to stay on for dinner, to which he had not been invited. At a reception at the White House, Lyndon Johnson asked her to dance with him; she refused on the grounds that it would hurt her image in India. The president understood. He wanted to see 'no harm [come] to the girl' and sanctioned three million tons of wheat and nine million dollars of aid to India.

The only person on record who made derogatory references to Indira's looks and intelligence was her aunt, Vijaya Lakshmi Pandit. Indira never forgave her (or her daughters) for slighting her and denied her senior diplomatic assignments. Indira Gandhi never forgave anyone who said anything against her.

Indira Gandhi's greatest triumph was the way she handled the Bangladesh crisis, wherein all her skills came together. She made a complete fool of the Pakistanis. India was being flooded by refugees entering the country. She tried to garner international support and went around the world, telling people what was happening. When she realized that the crisis had to reach a climax, she proved very astute. It was perhaps on her advice that the Indian Army built up the Mukti Bahini. By the time that President General Yahya Khan realized what was happening and declared war, the Indian Army was well inside Bangladesh. In less than a fortnight, the Pakistani Army surrendered. It was, by all accounts, a masterful strategy, and Indira Gandhi very deservedly got the Bharat Ratna.

At the end of the crisis, *The Illustrated Weekly of India* was the only Indian journal to persist in pressuring the government to release the 93,000 Pakistani prisoners of war. I took a delegation of four members, including one-time Indian ambassador to the US Gaganbhai Mehta and the writers Khwaja Ahmed Abbas and Krishan Chandra, to call on Indira Gandhi in an attempt to facilitate the release of the prisoners. Mrs Gandhi snubbed Gaganbhai, calling him an American stooge, and silenced Abbas and Chandra. Then she turned on me and said that my writings were embarrassing her. I replied that the object of my exercise was indeed to embarrass her and I was glad to know that I was succeeding. She fixed me with a look of contempt and said, 'Mr Singh, you may regard yourself as a great editor. But let me tell you, you do not know the first thing about politics.' I said, 'Mrs Gandhi, what is morally wrong can never be politically right. Holding prisoners of war after the war is over is morally wrong.' She again turned her large, dark eyes on me. 'Thanks for lecturing me on morality,' she said and dismissed us. I was convinced that she would never speak to me again. But a few days later, when she was in Bombay, she sought me out at a large and crowded reception and chatted with me in a friendly manner. I knew then that I had driven my point home.

In 1975, with accusations of corruption in the government soaring and the Opposition calling for total revolution, the country was fast sliding into chaos. Every other day, there was a bandh of some kind. Schools and colleges stayed shut for days. Large processions marched through streets, smashing shop windows and wrecking cars. Indira Gandhi was driven to despair. Her position became further vulnerable when the Allahabad high court held her guilty of electoral malpractices and disqualified her from Parliament membership. Persuaded by advisors such as Siddhartha

Shankar Ray and Sanjay Gandhi, she imposed Emergency on the country. My attitude to the Emergency was ambivalent. I supported the move to clamp down on law-breakers (including Jayaprakash Narayan, whom I otherwise admired), but I felt that the censorship of the press would prove counter-productive as it would deprive editors like me, who supported Mrs Gandhi, of credibility. For three weeks, I did not publish *The Illustrated Weekly* and, when forced to resume publication, gave instructions that no photographs of Mrs Gandhi or her ministers were to be used. I was treated gently, as I was regarded a friend by Mrs Gandhi and Sanjay, and summoned to Delhi to meet her. I had my say, protesting against the censorship, and told her before leaving, 'My family is sure that if I spoke my mind you would have me locked up.' She smiled and bade me goodbye. *The Weekly* was treated as a special case and I published articles by critics of the Emergency and pleaded for the release of political prisoners.

There was, as I have said, a strong streak of vengefulness in Indira Gandhi. A lot of people who were jailed during the Emergency were victims of the spite of the Gandhis. Despite repeated requests and pleas for the release of such prisoners, Mrs Gandhi refused to relent—including in the case of Bhim Sen

Sachar, ex-chief minister of Punjab, then in his seventies. One thing that Indira Gandhi did not suffer from was compassion. Her pettiness was particularly evident in her dealings with her younger daughter-in-law, Maneka. After Sanjay—whom Mrs Gandhi both loved and feared—died, she made Maneka unwelcome in her home and showed a marked preference for Sonia.

Another characteristic she developed after years of being in power was to snub people who least expected to be. At my repeated requests, she agreed to see Kewal Singh, who had been her foreign secretary and ambassador in Washington. Then she proceeded to give him a dressing down till he broke down. She did the same to Jagat Mehta, whose posting as ambassador to Germany she cancelled after it had been accepted.

When it came to Operation Bluestar, I believe Indira Gandhi was misled. From my years of acquaintance with her, I know that she had no prejudice at all against any community—not against Muslims, not against Sikhs. She consulted people about handling Bhindranwale and got contradictory advice from different sides. She didn't trust President Zail Singh, so she turned to the army. She was assured by senior officials that once the army went in and surrounded the Golden Temple, no fight would be put up and

Bhindranwale would surrender. I know that when she went to the temple two or three days after the operation, she was horrified because bodies were still floating in the sarovar and there were bloodstains that were being cleaned up. She turned to Major General K.S. Brar and asked, 'What is all this?' She had believed the army when she was told that there would be no fighting.

I was still a Member of Parliament when Mrs Gandhi was assassinated on the morning of 31 October 1984. Despite my differences with her, I was deeply distressed to hear of her dastardly murder at the hands of her own security guards, both Sikhs. She had many shortcomings, but perhaps that alone was what made her human. She may not have been a likeable person, but she was, in her own way, a woman to be loved and admired.

MOTHER TERESA

It has been more than thirty years since I was asked to do a profile of Mother Teresa for the *New York Times*. I wrote to Mother Teresa seeking her permission to call on her. Having got it, I spent three days with her, from the early hours of the morning to late at night. Nothing in my journalistic career has remained as sharply etched in my memory as those three days with her in Calcutta.

Before I met her, I read Malcolm Muggeridge's book on her, *Something Beautiful for God*. Malcolm was a recent convert to Catholicism and prone to believing in miracles. He had gone to make a film on Mother Teresa for the BBC. They first went to the Nirmal Hriday Home for dying destitutes close to the Kalighat temple. The team took some shots of the building from outside and of its sunlit courtyard. The camera crew was of the opinion that the interior was too dark and they had no lights that would help them take the shots they needed.

However, since some footage was left over, they decided to use it for interior shots. When the film was developed later, the shots of the dormitories inside were found to be clearer and brighter than those taken in sunlight. The first thing I asked Mother Teresa was if this was true. 'But of course,' she replied. 'Such things happen all the time.' Then she added with greater intensity: 'Every day, every hour, every single minute, God manifests Himself in some miracle.'

She narrated other miracles of the days when her organization was little known and always short of cash. 'Money has never been much of a problem,' she told me. 'God gives through His people.' She told me that when she started her first school in the slums, she had no more than five rupees with her. But as soon as people came to know what she was doing, they brought money and other things.

The first institution she took me to was Nirmal Hriday. It was in 1952 that the Calcutta Corporation had handed over the building to her. Orthodox Hindus were outraged. Four hundred Brahmin priests attached to the Kali temple gathered outside the building. 'One day, I went out and spoke to them. "If you want to kill me, kill me. But do not disturb the inmates. Let them die in peace." That silenced them. Then one of the priests staggered in. He was in an advanced stage of galloping phthisis. The nuns looked after him till he died.' That changed the priests' attitude towards Mother Teresa. Later, one day, another priest entered the home, prostrated himself at her feet and said, 'For thirty years, I have served the Goddess Kali in her temple. Now the Goddess stands before me.'

On my way back, Mother Teresa dropped me at the Dum Dum Airport. As I was about to take leave of her, she said, 'So?' She wanted to know if I had anything else to ask her. 'Tell me, how can you touch people with loathsome diseases like leprosy and gangrene? Aren't you revolted by people filthy with dysentery and cholera vomit?'

'I see Jesus in every human being,' Mother Teresa replied. 'I say to myself, this is hungry Jesus. This one has gangrene, dysentery or cholera. I must wash him and tend to him.'

I wrote a humble tribute to her for the *New York Times* and put her on the cover of *The Illustrated Weekly*. Till then, she was little known outside Calcutta; after that, more people got to know about her work. She sent me a short note of thanks, which I have in a silver frame in Kasauli. It is among my most valued possessions. It says: 'I am told you do not believe in God. I send you God's blessings.'

I have often thought about those three days I spent with Mother Teresa in Calcutta. We walked through crowded streets, rode in trams to visit her various hospitals, crèches for abandoned children and homes for the dying. I still remember how she tended to a very ill man who was dying. She was with him, looking after him, all the time telling him: 'Bhogoban achhen'—God is there. The way in which Mother Teresa went about looking after and tending to the sick, the dying, the hungry—it was the same as Bhagat Puran Singh.

Some years later, during one of my trips to Calcutta, I requested Mother Teresa to meet me. But she declined, saying that she would not come to my hotel room. It was okay by me, because I respected her. I saw her last when she was in Delhi. She had come here when H.S. Sikand (of Sikand Motors) had gifted a van for her Missionaries of Charity, but this time she did not seem to recognize me. I smiled and greeted her; though she did smile back, she did so in the way you do when you don't really recognize a person.

SHRADDHA MATA

It was during my editorship of the fortnightly journal *New Delhi* that I first met Shraddha Mata. I did a long feature article on the tantric sadhvi who, according to M.O. Matthai, had borne Prime Minister Nehru an illegitimate child. In the process, I became quite friendly with her. Whenever I was in Jaipur, I called on her at her permanent abode, Hathroi Fort. It was no longer the journalistic nosiness to probe into her past association with Pandit Nehru. It was more a spirit of adventure to explore the world in which she lived and of which I knew nothing: of round-the-clock prayer, the tantric rites amongst burning corpses and her down-to-earth earthiness.

Shraddha Mata was already in her mid-seventies

when I met her, and the most beautiful woman of her age you would see anywhere. What she must have looked like in her twenties when she turned a tantric! She was the stuff dreams are made of: hair knotted in a bun, ivory complexion, high cheekbones, full bosom. A tiger skin to cover her middle and Shiva's trident in her hand. She lived alone in Hathroi Fort. She spent most of her day meditating in a tiny windowless cell dug in the ramparts of the fort. The lookout tower had been converted into a shrine to the Goddess Durga; there, she kept vigil till the early hours, performing tantric rituals and weird ceremonials while the world slept.

The fortress was infested with snakes and scorpions. Also mice and mosquitoes. She refused to let anyone kill them—taking life, according to her, was God's prerogative. Her closest companions were a pack of friendly dogs, all jet-black. During the day, Shraddha Mata sometimes received visitors seated on her takht posh, crown dais, draped in saffron robes; the visitors would have to squat uncomfortably on the bare floor, her dogs sprawled between her and them. On one visit, she said to me: 'Tell people of Mahashakti of the third eye, through which Truth is revealed. Warn the people against pursuing materialism; it will spell the ruin of the world.' She talked of the Kendra Bindu and the teachings of the saints. She turned to the conjunction of the planets and their effect on humans. 'If only Sanjay had come to see me as I had asked him to do, I would have given him a jap that would have saved his life. I met Sanjay only once, when he was holidaying with his family in Kashmir. He was then a little boy. I could see in his eyes that he was going to be tejasvi (radiant personality). Sanjay's son, Varun, is destined to be the reviver of Hinduism. Once I told Panditji that he was destroying the sacred threads of the Hindus, his grandson would put them back.'

On another occasion, I touched her feet and asked about her health. She told me about her diabetes.

'It was the water in England that brought it on,' she said. 'I was there to inaugurate a Shakti temple in Sussex. They put me on insulin.' The diabetes had affected her vision. At times, it brought a high fever. 'One day, it shot up to 105,' she said. 'Medicines did not help. I brought it down to normal by chanting the right mantra.' She read disbelief in my eyes and decided to cut me to size: 'The first time you came to see me at Nigambodh Ghat, I called you an "ulloo ka pattha". You put it down in your column in English as "son of an owl".' She laughed at her own joke.

That was the tenor of all our meetings.

PROTIMA BEDI

∽

The two words missing from Protima Bedi's life's lexicon were 'no' and 'regret'. She could never say no to a man who desired her, and grew into a very desirable and animated young woman—whom most men found irresistible. And she did not regret any of the emotional and physical experiences she had.

Protima felt that keeping secrets was like lying, so she told everyone everything, including her husband and the succession of lovers who entered her life. She broke up marriages but remained blissfully unaware of the hurt she caused people. She had to get everything off her ample bosom.

Protima Gauri (as she renamed herself) had a zest for living. She loved men, liquor and drugs. She had an enormous appetite for sex and admitted to enjoying it as many as six times a day. She had a large range of lovers. Protima hated humbugs and hypocrites. She wrote: 'Every woman I know secretly longed to have many lovers but stopped herself for many reasons. I had the capacity to love many at a time and for this had been called shallow and wayward and a good-time girl.'

Protima also had a puckish sense of humour. Once, she arrived in Bombay with an electric vibrator. A very scandalized customs officer refused to let it pass. She gave him a dressing down: 'My husband is out of town most of the time—what do you expect me to do? I am trying to be faithful! Are you encouraging infidelity?' She got away with it.

Death caught Protima unawares. She was killed in a landslide while on a pilgrimage to Badrinath. And on the same day, in Bombay, died Persis Khambatta, India's first beauty queen and the one-time mistress of Protima's husband, Kabir Bedi.

ACKNOWLEDGEMENTS

The literary estate of Khushwant Singh and the publishers thank Penguin Books India for permission to reprint the following copyright material:

'Georgine' from *Delhi: A Novel*, 'Yasmeen' from *The Company of Women*, 'Nooran' from *Train to Pakistan*, and 'Portrait of a Lady' from *Collected Stories*.